William Shakespeare

THE LIFE OF
HENRY V

William Shakespeare

THE LIFE OF
HENRY V

Editor
Annalisa Castaldo
Widener University

Series Editor
James H. Lake
Louisiana State University,
Shreveport

ISBN: 978-1-58510-161-0
ISBN 10: 1-58510-161-3

Printed in the United States of America

10 9 8 7 6 5 4 3 2 1

1006TS

TABLE OF CONTENTS

Introduction to the Kittredge Edition   vii

Introduction to the Focus Edition   xi

The Life of Henry V   1

How to Read *Henry V* as Performance   107

Timeline   111

Topics for Discussion and Further Study   114

Bibliography   117

Filmography   120

Publisher's Note

George Lyman Kittredge's insightful editions of Shakespeare have endured in part because of his eclecticism, his diversity of interests, and his wide-ranging accomplishments — all of which are reflected in the valuable notes in each volume. The plays in the *New Kittredge Shakespeare* series retain the original Kittredge notes and introductions, changed or augmented only when some modernization seems necessary. These new editions also include introductory essays by contemporary editors, notes on the plays as they have been performed on stage and film, and additional student materials.

These plays are being made available by Focus Publishing with the permission of the Kittredge heirs.

Ron Pullins, Publisher
Newburyport, 2006

INTRODUCTION TO THE KITTREDGE EDITION

HENRY THE FIFTH is mentioned in the Stationers' Register on August 4, 1600, and the formal entry, by Thomas Pavyer, comes ten days later.[1] The First Quarto (1600) offers a garbled text of a drastically cut-down version. The Second Quarto (1602) was printed from the First; and so, apparently, was the Third, which, though dated 1608, was in fact published in 1619. The First Folio contains the play in its full and authentic form.[2] Bad as it is, the First Quarto enables one to correct a good many of the Folio's misprints. Three lines not found in the Folio appear to be genuine and are supplied from the Quarto in the present text (ii, 1, 110–111; iv, 3, 48). The most famous of all Shakespearean emendations is Theobald's correction of the Folio reading 'and a Table of greene fields' (ii, 3, 17), which makes no sense, to 'and 'a babbled of green fields.' The Quartos omit the words.

The date of HENRY THE FIFTH is fixed with unusual exactness by the reference to Essex in the Chorus to Act V:

> Were now the general of our gracious Empress
> (As in good time he may) from Ireland coming,
> Bringing rebellion broached on his sword,
> How may would the peaceful city quit
> To welcome him!

Essex left London on March 27, 1599, reached Dublin in April, and, returning from a campaign which was a complete fiasco, arrived at London on September 28

Editor's Note: I have largely retained the Kittredge introduction, eliminating only out-of-date scholarship and some long quotes from Shakespeare's sources. All explanatory footnotes are mine.

1   In 16th and 17th century England, all plays had to be registered with and approved by the government. The office that was in charge of this was called the Stationers' Register.

2   Quartos are cheaply bound single editions of plays, roughly equivalent to paperbacks today. Folios are large, expensive books, like coffee table books. The First Folio was printed in 1623, 9 years after Shakespeare's death, as a memorial, and contains versions of all his plays. Sometimes the Folio versions differ dramatically from the Quarto versions, and modern editors have to compare the two and decide which version they should present to their readers. This edition is based on the Folio version of *Henry V*.

in the same year.[3] Meres, in his *Palladis Tamia,* published in the autumn of 1598, mentions *Henry the Fourth,* but not HENRY THE FIFTH. The play is promised in the Epilogue to *Henry the Fourth, Part II.*

For history Shakespeare relies for the most part on Holinshed's *Chronicle.*[4] *The Famous Victories of Henry the Fifth* includes most of the reign, ending with the betrothal to Katherine of France, which took place on May 21, 1420.[5] From this play Shakespeare took hints for the action and he sometimes echoes its phrases. Thus, In the famous anecdote of the tennis balls (i, 2, 234 ff.), the king's eloquent reply to the Dauphin's insulting message is quite original; but there are traces of both Holinshed and the [anonymous] play.

The French nobles are not well treated by Shakespeare. Their rather vulgar frivolity is distasteful to the modern reader, who looks at the situation impartially, and not with the eyes of a patriotic Elizabethan. Holinshed tells us simply that the French, confident of victory, 'made great triumph; for the capteins had determined before how to diuide the spoile, and the soldiers the night before had plaid the Englishmen at dice.' The old play dramatizes Holinshed. It brings in three soldiers and a drummer playing at dice and speaking broken English; also a captain who has 'set three or foure chaire makers a worke, to make a new disguised chaire to set that womanly King of England in, that all the people may laugh and scoffe at him.' Yet he pities the 'poore English scabs': 'Why, take an English man out of his warme bed and his stale drinke, but one moneth, and alas what wil become of him? But giue the Frenchman a Reddish roote, and he wil liue with it all the dayes of his life.' (Cf. iii, 7, 93, 158 ff.; iv, Chorus, 17–22.) Alençon is of much the same opinion in *1 Henry VI,* i, 2, 9–12:

> They want their porridge and their fat bull-beeves.
> Either they must be dieted like mules
> And have their provender tied to their mouths,
> Or piteous they will look, like drowned mice.

The way in which Shakespeare picked up phrases is well illustrated in the Prologue:

> Then should the warlike Harry, like himself,
> Assume the port of Mars, and at his heels
> (Leash'd in, like hounds) should famine, sword, and fire
> Crouch for employment.

---

3   The Earl of Essex was a nobleman and a favorite of the Queen. He believed Elizabeth should marry him, so that he would be king. After he returned from his campaign to subdue the Irish, he attempted to revolt against Elizabeth and take the throne. This attempt failed and he was executed.

4   Raphael Holinshed's *Chronicles of England, Scotland and Ireland,* was written in 1577 and revised in 1587. It served as Shakespeare's main source for this play, although he also appears to have consulted the earlier history by Edward Hall, *The Union of the Two Noble and Illustre Families of Lancaster and York,* written in 1548 and revised in 1550.

5   This anonymous play was entered in the Stationers' Register on May 14, 1594, 6 years before Shakespeare wrote his version.

In Holinshed King Henry uses a similar figure in reply to an ambassador from the besieged citizens of Rouen: 'He declared that the goddesse of battell, called *Bellona*, had three handmaidens, euer of necessitie attending vpon her, as blood, fire, and famine.' Cf. also the exhortation of the Archbishop of Canterbury (i, 2, 131): 'With blood and sword and fire to win your right.' Canterbury's long address in explanation of King Henry's title to the crown of France (i, 2, 35–100) is simply versified from Holinshed, with only such slight changes as are needed to transfer prose into blank verse. Indeed, Shakespeare found in Holinshed's prose four or five lines which he could take over as verse without the change of a word.

The Quarto omits the Prologue and all other speeches of the Chorus. Some of these furnish historical information that the audience cannot do without. Incidentally, they are interesting documents in the history of dramatic criticism. They express, over and over again, the doctrine of the voluntary subjection of our minds to the illusion of the stage (as opposed to dramatic deception)—a principle which a succession of eminent critics arrived at by a long course of study and debate, and which Schlegel and Coleridge are often thought to have finally worked out.

The character of Henry V in this play is inconsistent with the character of the Prince in *Henry the Fourth*. The difference is not moral, but mental. The Prince has a brilliant intellect that works with flashing rapidity; King Henry's mind is not inferior, but it is of another order: it is strong and sure, but does not scintillate. No such mental transformation could result from a reform in manners and morals. The inconsistency is, of course, in no sense a fault in Shakespeare's portrayal. He was quite at liberty to give different accounts of the same personage in different plays. For the intensely religious nature of King Henry, Shakespeare had ample justification in Holinshed, and he has emphasized it throughout, so that the conquest of France becomes to all intents and purposes a holy war.[6]

George Lyman Kittredge
1939

---

6   Modern scholarship has tended to emphasize the moral ambiguity of the war as Shakespeare presents it, and to see the character of Henry V as equally complex, as opposed to the idea of the hero-King fighting a justified Holy War accepted by scholars in the first half of the twentieth century.

INTRODUCTION TO THE FOCUS EDITION

Henry V is the capstone and pinnacle of the eight-play cycle Shakespeare composed concerning the Wars of the Roses (1422-1485) and the events that led up to those wars (1399-1420). The period, and the plays, begin with the reign of Richard II, who was deposed by his cousin Henry in 1399. This single event–the forcible overthrow of a divinely appointed king–set off a chain reaction that led to more depositions, civil war and eventually the rise of the Tudors, the family who ruled England during most of Shakespeare's lifetime.

Although historically Henry V's reign falls in the exact center of this period, Shakespeare saved this king for last. Henry V was the only king during this period who both inherited the throne from his father and successfully passed it on to his son. He was also the most successful military leader, conquering all of France. For the Elizabethans, Henry V was a shining symbol, untouched by the scandal of his father, who took the throne by force, and not responsible for the civil war that erupted during his son's reign.

Three of the four plays in the second tetralogy (*Henry IV:1* and *2* and *Henry V*) chronicle the education, development and success of this single figure, Henry, first as Prince of Wales and then as king. Given the focus on Henry and his undeniable military success (both in history and in the play), many critics have seen the play as a celebratory epic that uncomplicatedly praises Henry as the perfect warrior-king. But the play is darker and more ambiguous than that, and there are episodes—treason by three trusted nobles, Henry's threats to brutalize the citizens of Harfluer, his prayer to God to "think not" on his father's usurpation of the throne, and his order to kill the French prisoners—that make Henry a complicated, even negative figure. In addition, many of the comic scenes, not to mention the plotting of Canterbury and Ely in 1.1, deflate or parody the epic claims of both Henry and the Chorus.

As Norman Rabkin argues in his important essay, "Rabbits, Ducks and *Henry V*" what is necessary is not to decide whether the play is heroic and epic, or ambiguous and satirical, but to recognize that it is both, often at exactly the same time. History itself reinforces this duality. Henry may have successfully kept the peace at home and conquered France, but his legacy was not a lasting one. In Shakespeare's own time the political situation was increasingly unstable. The aging queen (she would die three years after *Henry V* was written) refused to name a successor, and while the Chorus celebrates the Earl of Essex's campaign against Ireland in his first speech, very soon after the play was first performed, Essex would return in disgrace, his campaign a complete failure, and attempt to take the throne by force. Like the rest of his peers, Shakespeare's view of monarchs and military power would have been decidedly complex.

The play presents complex investigations on other themes as well. For a play that is almost entirely about war, battle itself is conspicuously absent. The only actual confrontation of a French fighter and an English fighter is 4.4, a comic scene in which a terrified Frenchman surrenders immediately to the money-grubbing Pistol. There are no duels, no acts of heroism; in fact, the audience never sees Henry draw his sword. Instead, it is the effects of war that we see or hear about—towns devastated, children killed, soldiers preparing themselves to die and wondering if the cause is worth their lives. In the twentieth and twenty-first centuries, the costs of war and the reasons for declaring it have been continuously reexamined, making *Henry V* increasingly relevant by raising these very issues.

The play is also startlingly modern in its focus on language and the power language has to shape reality. In the world of advertising and George Orwell's doublespeak, everyone recognizes that truth is often less important than spin. Henry is the master of spin, and it is startling to realize how little actually *happens* in the play. Instead of fighting actual battles, Henry talks about them. He tells the Governor of Harfleur the horrors that will result if he does not surrender, and the Governor surrenders. He tells his outnumbered troops they will celebrate their victory every year, and the victory appears. Most remarkably, he tells the traitors who were set to assassinate him that they are bad people, and they not only agree, they rejoice in their capture and imminent death. Henry can literally create reality with his words. The Chorus, for all his apologies, is the only one to match Henry's linguistic ability, by evoking the power of the audience's imagination to create the world of the play.

Other characters do not have this power, but their use of language connects to issues of power, gender, class and nation. Characters speak with English accents or coarsely, or not at all. The further characters are from Henry's language, the less powerful they are, and the fewer choices open to them. *Henry V* dramatizes this repression while actually providing space for alterative voices. Henry may out-argue William, but the soldier's concerns about the war linger, and when the trick Henry plays on him is revealed, William eloquently defends himself. Pistol may be forced to abase himself to Fluellen, but the last word is his; alone on stage he laments his losses and determines to survive at any cost. Katherine may know all along that she must marry Henry, but she can make him woo her in her own language.

One voice, however, is silenced—the voice of Falstaff. The glorious wordsmith and mischievous companion to Prince Hal, banished at the end of *Henry IV:2*, dies offstage in *Henry V* and Pistol is a poor substitute. The chaotic energy and subversive wit of Falstaff cannot survive when Prince Hal actually becomes King Henry, and Shakespeare is right to let him go. Henry, and *Henry V,* are too powerful to be likable, as Falstaff made Prince Hal in *Henry IV.* There is little in *Henry V* of intimate human warmth and contact; Shakespeare intimates, in the conclusion to his investigation of history, that humanity is a flaw in the powerful, or perhaps that power is a flaw in humanity.

Performance History

From its very inception, *Henry V* was a play about performance itself. The insistent presence of the Chorus, continually reminding the audience of what cannot be shown and what they must therefore imagine, both denigrates and exalts the actual stage performance, pointing out how far any production is from reality, but celebrating the magical combination of rhetoric and imagination that is somehow more than reality could ever be. The major film productions of the play have celebrated this as well, providing thrilling battles, emotional music and moments of charged conflict. These moments are so powerful it is something of a shock to return to the original text and realize that they are not there. The charge of the French cavalry, Henry in a duel with this or that French noble, the Duke of York being overpowered and killed—none of these moments are played out in Shakespeare's original text; indeed, only the last is even described.

Whether deliberately or no, what Shakespeare created in *Henry V* was a work of immense malleability, a work which always reflects the beliefs of the director and audience and which provides so many performative options that it can easily be used to celebrate the British empire or to reject all war as evil. While other plays—*Macbeth, Romeo and Juliet* and *Hamlet*—are so well known they must be made fresh through innovative casting or staging, *Henry V* is unique in that it remains fresh precisely because it continually contradicts itself. Is it epic or sardonic? Is Henry a hero or a war criminal? Are the French arrogant cowards or noble victims? Each generation finds what it needs in the play.

The performance history of the play bears this out. *Henry V* exists in two very different forms: the Quarto of 1600 and the Folio of 1623. The Quarto version is only 1,600 lines long, half the length of the Folio, and does not have any of the Chorus's speeches, the opening scene between Canterbury and Eli, the Scots and Irish captains, Henry's speech "Once more unto the breach," the dialogue blaming the King for Falstaff's death (2.1), nor the second scene (4.2) with the French lords before the battle of Agincourt. These cuts make for a simpler, more straightforward play, more clearly celebratory and heroic. While we have no sure way of knowing which version was performed when, it seems clear that from the start the play was subject to cuts to clarify and simplify the themes.

Perhaps it was this ambiguity, or perhaps it was the topical nature (Joel Altman has convincingly argued that for Shakespeare's first audience, the French in *Henry V* were seen as a clear allegory for the Irish), but the play fell out of favor and was not revived, even in altered form, for well over a century. When it was restaged, it was dramatically altered to make its genre clear. One version was Charles Molloy's *The Half-Pay Officers: A Comedy* (1720) which focused on the comic adventures of

Fluellen and Macmorris. Another was *King Henry the Fifth: Or, the Conquest of France, By the English, A Tragedy* by Aaron Hill (1723). This version introduced Harriet, the niece of Lord Scroop and discarded mistress of Henry, who follows him to France and eventually kills herself in order to clear the way for the politically necessary marriage of Henry to Katherine.

While it was not unusual for Shakespeare's plays to be rewritten and "improved" in the seventeenth and eighteenth centuries, the wide variation in genre was unusual. Apparently directors as well as writers were not at all sure what Shakespeare had originally written: was it a tragedy? A comedy? A history? This uncertainty would continue throughout the eighteenth century, even after the play was staged in its original form in 1738. Although the play was staged with some regularity after that (although always with heavy cuts), it never reached the success of Shakespeare's tragedies, or even of *Henry IV:1*.

The play, however, became much more popular in the mid- and late nineteenth century thanks to the increased might of the British empire and a focus on spectacle and pageantry on stage. Henry himself became the symbol of British greatness, of the "little body with a mighty heart" (2.0.16), representing the courage, discipline and faith that allowed a small island to rule a mighty empire. And, ironically considering the Chorus's repeated reminders that the stage cannot "hold the vasty fields of France" (1.0.12), performances of *Henry V* became occasions for epic spectacle. In 1839 William Macready staged a version in which he starred, which involved seventy named actors, a variety of staged backdrops and Henry in plate armor. This began the pattern of expensive, elaborate shows: by 1859 Edmund Kean's production of *Henry V* ran over four hours because of the time required to shift the sets, and featured 200 extras and a triumphant processional before Act 5 (replacing the Chorus's description) with Kean on a white horse, seven standard-bearers, eight cannoneers and twenty-four archers. Quite obviously, by this point and for most of the rest of the century, the play had become an excuse for spectacle and speech-making, but little else.

Inevitably, there was a backlash against the increasing drive towards realism, and early twentieth century productions featured relative simplicity of staging and reduced numbers of extras. During the Boer War and World War I, the play received much less attention than it had during earlier British wars, such as the Crimean War. In 1915, Eric Williams produced a film entitled *England's Warrior King*, which featured scenes of the Royal Scots Greys regiment with a voice-over narration derived from *Henry V*. However, there were no outstanding productions of note, and this no doubt reflects the hollowness of patriotic spectacle when set against trench warfare.

In the second half of the twentieth century, the play was most often seen on stage as part of a sequence with *Richard II, Henry IV:1* and *2*. This allowed audiences to get to know Prince Hal before he became Henry, and measure the change that the role of king demanded. With the earlier plays' focus on Falstaff, the references to him in *Henry V* became more meaningful and poignant. The BBC also created several TV productions of *Henry V*, culminating in the version produced as part of the BBC/Time Life Shakespeare plays. First broadcast in 1979, this version featured

David Gwillim as Henry, reprising his role from *Henry IV:1* and *Henry IV:2*. The series' ability to have actors repeat their roles from play to play emphasized often missed echoes, especially in the character of Henry, as he grew and matured, shifting everything from clothes to style of speaking. The relationship between Henry and the characters he rejects along with Falstaff was especially poignant since these characters reappear, and die, in *Henry V*. There were some innovative moments–the Chorus interacted with a number of the characters, catching a tennis ball after the French Ambassador's visit, for example–but the productions were also hampered by the dictates of the series: almost no cuts, simple staging and basic camera work meant that the shows had the feel of a theatrical production without the energy of a live performance.

None of the television productions were especially innovative, but the sheer number speaks to the popularity of the play, especially after the release of Laurence Olivier's film in 1944. In modern times, the play continues to be performed, often with an anti-war slant. Whatever focus the director chooses for the play, audiences and reviewers seem compelled to read it against current politics. References to the play even appeared in the 2004 American presidential campaign, with John Kerry referencing the "band of brothers" speech to describe his Vietnam War experience.

Olivier and Branagh: Films of *Henry V*

In 1944, Laurence Olivier was given release time by the Royal Air Force to direct and star in a film of *Henry V*. While the production was not an overt propaganda film, it was designed to improve morale among the troops. How did the war affect Olivier's filming of *Henry V* ? First, it influenced his very choice of films. Olivier chose to film one of Shakespeare's plays not only because Shakespeare was the pride and joy of all England, but also because the Shakespeare's time—especially the reign of Elizabeth I (1558-1603)—represented the glory days of "Merrie Olde England," Furthermore, Olivier chose to film this particular play because it featured an almost miraculous battle—the battle of Agincourt—where the tired and sick English (numbering around 6,000) defeated a French army numbering 20,000 -30,000. Not only did the English win, but their losses were minor: not 29, as Shakespeare tells, but probably around a hundred to the French's 7,000 - 11,000. This was the story to tell the outnumbered British soldiers in the latter days of WWII.

The war, on some level, dictated the cuts Olivier made in the text. While the original would have had to be cut anyway to make a commercially viable film, the desire to present Henry as a purely noble and righteous king and his cause as "all unspotted" influenced what was cut out. Almost all non-comic material that cast a negative light on Henry or suggested a lack of unity was removed: the traitors who are hired by France to assassinate Henry, Henry's brutal threats of rape and pillage to the Governor of Harfleur, the hanging of Bardolph for stealing a church icon, Henry's order to kill the French prisoners and his rather condescending practical joke on William are all gone. In addition, the first two scenes, which show the Archbishop of Canterbury and the Bishop of Ely plotting to use the war to divert the King from taxing the church, are played for laughs, thus negating the effect.

This is not to suggest that Olivier reduced Henry to a cardboard cutout and the play to a celebration of war. The scene before Agincourt, when Henry talks to his soldiers in disguise, listens to their fears and debates internally on his course of action, is played fully and seriously, as is the speech of the Duke of Burgundy on the horrors of war. But a conscious effort is made to present Henry's course as the right one, the war as justified and those fighting it as unified.

What stands out even now about the film is the style, or rather styles, of filming. Olivier was a reluctant convert to Shakespeare on film; he did not believe the rhetorical and linguistic style of Shakespeare could transfer successfully to film. When he came to film *Henry V*, Olivier began with the Chorus' request to the audience: "let us, ciphers to this great accompt,/On your imaginary forces work" and divided the film into three levels of reality.

The first level, which opens and closes the film, is not the reality of Henry V, but of Elizabeth I: not with the preparation for a war, but the preparation for a play—the opening of *Henry V*. We are part of Shakespeare's original audience, but we are a special, privileged part, as the camera takes up backstage, to see the boy actors dress as women and catch a glimpse of Olivier playing James Burbage (the leading actor in Shakespeare's company) preparing to play Henry. In addition to allowing the film audience to adjust to the language and customs of Shakespeare's play, the long shot of London and the lively bustling theater provide a picture to wartime Britain of what London was and will be again. How strange, but how reassuring it must have been to see, not the bombed and half-destroyed London of 1944, but the pristine and comfortable London of 1600.

The French scenes represent a second level of reality, and while we are now "inside" the story rather than watching a play, this is still a level based in art rather than history. The scenes in France, especially those in the French court, are based on a series of medieval paintings, one for each month of the year, collectively known as the *Tres Riches Heures de Duc du Berry*. Indeed, the scene after the battle of Agincourt reproduces the picture for February with amazing precision, while the month of January is copied for the French court banquet.

Only in the Agincourt scenes does Olivier approach what might be considered the standard realism of film, with actual horses running full speed across real fields, and men fighting each other in what appears, mostly, to be real time. However, once again, Olivier was not about to create a "realistic" battle. There is no blood shed in the battle of Agincourt; in fact, the film deliberately references the 1938 Errol Flynn film *The Adventures of Robin Hood*, with men leaping out of trees, and Olivier's version partakes of its predecessor's atmosphere of boyish excitement. Olivier also adds a completely gratuitous but deeply satisfying duel between Henry and the Constable of France (the only Frenchman with real courage and honor). Mounted on opposing black and white steeds, Henry and the Constable fight the classic duel, with the Constable knocking away Henry's sword and apparently securing the victory, only to be stopped when Henry flattens him with a single manly punch.

In 1989, when Kenneth Branagh followed in Olivier's footsteps by starring in and directing his own version of *Henry V*, the world was very different. Olivier was an acknowledged star of stage and screen; Branagh was, at 28, a successful stage actor, but practically unknown on screen. Olivier's film was filmed during World War II; Branagh's film was a reaction to the Vietnam and Falkland Islands conflicts. And Branagh was reacting to and measuring himself against the immensely successful Olivier film, rather than breaking entirely new ground. Yet Branagh's version was as successful as Olivier's in many ways, and helped launch a new wave of Shakespearean films that may have crested but has not disappeared entirely. Opinion on Branagh's film has been mixed since the first reviews, but its influence cannot be doubted.

Branagh set out to make an all together darker film than Olivier. He restored the three conspirators and threats at Harfleur, executed Bardolph on screen and filmed a muddy, bloody scrum of a battle. Rather than play the two clerics for laughs, Branagh set the tone with the two men secretly whispering in a back room as they plot to use war as distraction from domestic events. But Branagh did not want to make his king a war criminal. Instead, his film clearly draws from the line of post-Vietnam films which range from *Born on the Fourth of July* to *Rambo* that aim to show more or less graphically that war is hell, but also a way to build character. Branagh's Henry begins the film a very young man, only partly in control of his court and ends a self-confident, inspiring king. While the audience is shown again and again the physical and emotional toll war takes on Henry, this only makes victory–political and personal–sweeter. Therefore, Branagh, with Olivier and many stage directors, cuts the most unforgivable of Henry's acts: ordering the killing of the prisoners and humiliating the honest soldier Williams.

Branagh, unlike Olivier, was not concerned with finding a filmic style to match Shakespeare's language; instead he was determined to make, as he puts it, "a truly popular film...utterly accessible to anyone of whatever age and background" (Branagh 10). He therefore not only chose realism but invested heavily in the secondary characters. Throughout the film, when Henry is speaking, the camera seeks out characters like Fluellen, Gower and Jamy, even before they speak any lines, so that the idea of a "band of brothers" is literalized by the time Agincourt takes place.

Branagh also wanted to make the importance of Falstaff and Henry's past life crystal clear, so he inserted several flashbacks into the movie. The first takes place during 2.1, after news of Falstaff's illness reaches Pistol, Nym and Bardolph; the second just before the on-stage execution of Bardolph. Both are drawn from *Henry IV:1* and give life to the relationship between the young Prince Hal and the disreputable companions that he was forced to reject when he became king. During Burgundy's speech about peace in 5.2, the camera focuses on Henry and then a series of memories appear, tallying the English dead. They begin with Henry's cousin, the Duke of York, and end, curiously, with Falstaff. The suggestion is that the dead are Henry's private losses and the whole tone of the film is a carefully balanced consideration of whether or not the great gains–Katherine, France, Henry's more secure grip on his own throne–are worth what had to be given up, especially since, as the Chorus reminds us, none of the victories would last.

A comparison of stills from these two scenes is instructive in many ways, especially in demonstrating the flexibility of the play as a whole. From the very beginning, for example, Olivier and Branagh make their themes clear through the respective presentations of the Chorus. Olivier, as mentioned above, starts his film at the Elizabethan premier of *Henry V*. His Chorus not only enters some six minutes after the film has started, but enters onto an Elizabethan stage, dressed as an Elizabethan gentleman (see figure 1). The overall effect is one of lightness and fun, emphasized by the theater audience's enthusiastic applause. Branagh, on the other hand, begins with the Chorus dressed in a dark overcoat specific to no particular period, lighting a match and intoning "O for a muse of fire" against a black backdrop. The tone is solemn and a bit mysterious and this continues as Branagh continually places the Chorus in proximity to danger or tragedy. The Chorus speaks from the trenches around Harfleur, flinching at explosions, and trudges after Henry's army, pulling his coat tight against the rain. Whereas Olivier's Chorus becomes less and less corporeal–finally becoming just a voice–Branagh's becomes more and more part of the events as he shivers against the cold, stumbles in the mud and, finally, ends the film by closing the door on the betrothal scene after his final soliloquy. Olivier's Chorus emphasizes our separation from history, Branagh's our connection to it.

The battle scenes, of course, differ radically. Neither is historically accurate, neither reflects Shakespeare's actual text and therefore these scenes, in many ways, reflect most clearly what the directors hoped to achieve. Olivier deliberately rejects realism and horror for clean fun and Hollywood excitement. Even at the most intense moments of fighting, there is no blood and no sign of pain (see figure 2). The battle even appears to be decided by a duel between Henry and the Constable of France, suggesting that Henry has single-handedly won France. Furthermore, the French (except for the Constable) are presented as arrogant cowards, boasting and drinking before the battle, and fleeing the fighting for the easier target of the young boys guarding the tents.

Branagh rejects this comfortable vision of war and instead presents a battle of mud, rain and brutality. Men are shown being drowned, stabbed in the back and dying from broken necks, rather than duelling heroically with swords. Many of the battle scenes are actually devoted to the struggles of the secondary characters rather than Henry (see figure 3), so that a whole range of reactions to war are visible. In the end Branagh films Henry carrying the dead Boy through the wasteland of bodies and mud as a sort of penance for causing so much suffering, but also as a demonstration that only personal leadership can make such suffering worthwhile.

Henry V is a play about war and therefore there are few roles for women. However, the play is deeply concerned with issues of gender and these issues work their way into various productions through the character of the French princess, Katherine. In the first scene with Katherine–the language scene–the two directors clearly signal their very different views. Olivier presents a fairytale princess cutting roses in a garden that seems completely removed from the war. The language lesson is nothing more than a way to pass the time. Branagh, on the other hand, opens with Katherine tending to her doves (a sign of peace) and the strain is evident on her face from the beginning.

He stands to address the rest of the army one final time before leading them into battle.

HENRY V
Now, soldiers, march away;
And how thou pleasest, God, dispose the day!

At last the time has come to move out to prepare for the start of the fight. Henry leads his men as they go down on their knees to cross themselves and kiss the ground upon which they will fight. A final prayer.

English Lines: day

From behind some stakes, the Chorus emerges and begins to walk towards us as soldiers run past him towards the battlefield.

CHORUS
And so our scene must to the battle fly;
Where, O for pity! We shall much disgrace
With four or five most vile and ragged foils,
Right ill-disposed in brawl ridiculous
The name of Agincourt.

As he exits, we cut to:

French and English Lines: day

A montage sequence as both sides prepare for the battle. The French nobles, confident of victory with their greater numbers, mount their horses and prepare their weapons. It is the Constable who will give the order for the battle to commence and they watch him anxiously for his signal.

On the other side, the worried English nobles try to hide their fear. Exeter, Westmoreland and Erpingham patrol the line of stakes, encouraging the soldiers. Gloucester and Bedford prepare their horses.

Henry too mounts his beautiful white horse, appearing calm and confident for his men. Exeter, now mounted, is handed his mace by Erpingham.

The bowmen are lined up and under the watchful eye of Gower and Jamy prepare their bows for the onslaught.

At last the Constable lowers the visor of his helmet and with a great flourish of his arm, signals for the French charge to begin.

We hear the sound of thousands of horses galloping towards the   101

A page from Branagh's published version of his screenplay. The text from the original play is in bold, but just as important is the description of the scene and the characters' emotions, which help flesh out the story. From *Henry V* by William Shakespeare, adapted by Kenneth Branagh, published by Chatto & Windus. Reprinted by permission of The Random House Group Ltd.

She undertakes to learn English because she knows she has to. The lesson gradually becomes silly fun, but that is abruptly cut short when Katherine opens her door to see her brother and father on their way to a war council, and she too falls silent

In the final scene, when Henry woos Katherine, the differences between Olivier and Branagh are more subtle, but still worth noting. In the stills provided, the Henrys are very similar—both lean down to a seated Katherine from above, physically dominating the shot. Both are richly dressed and look serious but also slightly amused by this task of winning the heart of a princess. The difference is in the portrayal of Katherine. Renée Asherson plays Katherine as a flirt, coyly smiling at Henry (see figure 4). She is happy to be wooed by the English king and wants only to make him work a little to prove his love. Emma Thompson, on the other hand (see figure 5), plays a serious Katherine who knows she has no choice in this marriage, and is trying to work out how she can marry "de enimie of France." Their relationship is altogether less certain, and it is instructive that during Henry's final speech, she refuses to look up until the very last minute. Even then, she does not smile. Olivier returns his audience triumphantly to the Globe, where his Katherine revels in the audience's applause, and then he cuts the final, somber Chorus speech. Branagh's serious and perhaps unwilling Katherine, on the other hand, leads naturally into the Chorus's somber reminder that the future holds only more war and loss. From first to last, then, each director supports his view of the play through choices in acting, costuming, and setting.

Adaptations

Henry V, unlike many of Shakespeare's popular plays, does not lend itself to adaptation, and there are no "teen" or "modern" versions, as there are with Romeo and Juliet, Macbeth or Taming of the Shrew. Orson Welles ends Chimes at Midnight, his adaptation of the two Henry IV plays, with a few lines borrowed from Henry V, but these are taken out of context. One use of the play, however, is worth noting. In the 1994 film, Renaissance Man, Danny DeVito plays an out-of-work advertising executive who ends up tutoring a bunch of army recruits (unrealistically, the army wants them to learn to think for themselves). DeVito spends most of the movie teaching the students Hamlet, but late in the film he takes them off base to see a production of Henry V. The film shows part of Henry's speech before Harfleur, intercut with shots of the rapt recruits. They are deeply moved and later, when one of the recruits is taunted to recite Shakespeare by the drill sergeant, he delivers the St. Crispin's day speech with enough conviction to win over the sergeant. While the film as a whole is not very good, it is intriguing to see how the script begins with the well known Hamlet but shifts to the much more martial Henry V when the recruits need to prove themselves. In this way, Renaissance Man is a good example of how most directors have treated Henry V, as a play that allows for the exploration of current views of war, manhood, sacrifice and maturity.

Annalisa Castaldo

2006

Editor's Note: Kittredge's editing and notes are generally a model of clarity and intelligence, and I have left them largely untouched. However, I have made a few changes. I have followed modern practice of italicizing foreign words and phrases, and I have added notes translating all of the French dialogue that is not already translated in the text. I have Americanized spellings throughout, as well as modernizing punctuation more completely than Kittredge did, to aid readers in understanding the text.

In addition to the French translations, I have added notes on some words or ideas Kittredge did not explain, as well as adding more detailed notes drawing the reader's attention to thematic elements of the play (these added notes are followed by [A.C.] to distinguish them from Kittredge's work). In the former case, Kittredge often assumed knowledge among his readers of historical, mythic or literary figures that is no longer common and should now be explained. In the latter case, I believe that editors should be willing to offer thematic guidance to readers, introducing points which may be overlooked, but which enrich the experience of the play. While I would never tell a reader that a scene has a particular or singular meaning, I do feel that part of modern editing is more than helping readers to understand definitions of individual words, it is helping readers to understand the play as a whole. [A.C.]

THE LIFE OF
HENRY THE FIFTH

DRAMATIS PERSONÆ

Chorus.
King Henry the Fifth.
Duke of Gloucester, } brothers to
Duke of Bedford, } the *King.*
Duke of Exeter, uncle to the *King.*
Duke of York, cousin to the *King.*
Earl of Salisbury.
Earl of Westmoreland.
Earl of Warwick.
Archbishop of Canterbury.
Bishop of Ely.
Earl of Cambridge.
Lord Scroop.
Sir Thomas Grey.
Sir Thomas Erpingham, } officers
Gower, an English captain, } in *King*
Fluellen, a Welsh captain, } *Henry's*
Macmorris, an Irish captain, } army.
Jamy, a Scottish captain,
John Bates, } soldiers in
Alexander Court, } the same.
Michael Williams, }
Pistol.
Nym.
Bardolph.

Boy.
A Herald.
Charles the Sixth, King of France.
Lewis, the Dauphin.
Duke of Burgundy.
Duke of Orleans.
Duke of Bourbon.
The Constable of France.
Rambures, }
Grandpré, } French lords.
Beaumont, }
Governor of Harfleur.
Montjoy, a French herald.
Ambassadors to the *King of England.*
Isabel, Queen of France.
Katherine, daughter to *Charles* and
Isabel.
Alice, a lady attending on her.
Hostess of the Boar's Head tavern
in Eastcheap (formerly *Mistress
Quickly,* now married to *Pistol*).
Lords, Ladies, Officers, Soldiers,
Citizens, Messengers, and
Attendants.

SCENE.—ENGLAND AND FRANCE.

Enter Prologue.

O for a Muse of fire, that would ascend[†]
The brightest heaven of invention,
A kingdom for a stage, princes to act,
And monarchs to behold the swelling scene!
Then should the warlike Harry, like himself,   5
Assume the port of Mars, and at his heels
(Leash'd in, like hounds) should famine, sword, and fire
Crouch for employment. But pardon, gentles all,
The flat unraised spirits that have dar'd
On this unworthy scaffold to bring forth   10
So great an object. Can this cockpit hold
The vasty fields of France? Or may we cram
Within this wooden O the very casques
That did affright the air at Agincourt?
O, pardon! since a crooked figure may   15
Attest in little place a million,
And let us, ciphers to this great accompt,
On your imaginary forces work.
Suppose within the girdle of these walls
Are now confin'd two mighty monarchies,   20
Whose high-upreared and abutting fronts
The perilous narrow ocean parts asunder.
Piece out our imperfections with your thoughts:
Into a thousand parts divide one man
And make imaginary puissance.   25
Think, when we talk of horses, that you see them
Printing their proud hoofs i' th' receiving earth.
For 'tis your thoughts that now must deck our kings,

PROLOGUE.
6. **port of Mars**: appearance of Mars, god of War. [A.C.] 8. **gentles:** gentlemen and ladies. 9. **flat unraised spirits:** uninspired intellects. 10. **scaffold.** The Elizabethan stage structure was unsubstantial, compared with that of the modern theater, and it projected into the auditorium (pit, or orchestra). Hence it might well be called a *scaffold.* The word also suggests the temporary platforms in the inn yards on which plays were presented before the first English theater was built and which some of the audience could still remember.—**Cockpit.** The theater was circular or octagonal, and the seats rose in tiers, so that it was not unlike the pits in which cockfights were held. 13. **the very casques.** The theater would be too small to hold 'even the helmets' worn at Agincourt. 16. **Attest:** stand for. 17. **this great accompt:** this great amount, or sum (i.e., the great subject which the actors are to set forth). 21. **upreared:** erected— **fronts:** foreheads, but also borders of the kingdoms. 25. **puissance:** forces, troops. The word is sometimes trisyllabic (as here), sometimes dissyllabic. 28. **deck.** i.e., with appropriate splendour of costume.

---

† Both modern film versions choose to keep the Chorus, despite the fact that movies can show the sweep and grandeur of the battlefield quite well. Their reasons for doing so, and the effect of retaining or dropping the Chorus, is an excellent introduction to the themes of the play. [A.C.]

Fig. 1: Olivier's Chorus on stage in Elizabethan England, in the first of several realities Olivier presents in his film. © United Artists / Photofest.

Carry them here and there, jumping o'er times,
Turning th' accomplishment of many years   30
Into an hourglass. For the which supply,
Admit me Chorus to this history,
Who, Prologue-like, your humble patience pray,
Gently to hear, kindly to judge our play.   *Exit.*

---

31. **For the which supply:** to fill up the defects just mentioned (i.e., by describing what the players cannot act or represent). 33. **Prologue-like:** in the guise of a Prologue, or in the manner of a Prologue—probably the former, the Prologue having a conventional costume.

Act One

SCENE I. [*London. An antechamber in the* King's *Palace.*]

Enter the two Bishops—[the Archbishop of] Canterbury
and [the Bishop of] Ely.

CANT.   My lord, I'll tell you, that self bill is urg'd
        Which in th' eleventh year of the last king's reign
        Was like, and had indeed against us pass'd
        But that the scambling and unquiet time
        Did push it out of farther question.   5

ELY   But how, my lord, shall we resist it now?

CANT.   It must be thought on. If it pass against us,
        We lose the better half of our possession;
        For all the temporal lands which men devout
        By testament have given to the Church   10
        Would they strip from us; being valu'd thus—
        As much as would maintain, to the King's honor,
        Full fifteen earls and fifteen hundred knights,
        Six thousand and two hundred good esquires,
        And, to relief of lazars and weak age,   15
        Of indigent faint souls, past corporal toil,
        A hundred almshouses right well supplied;
        And to the coffers of the King beside,
        A thousand pounds by th' year. Thus runs the bill.

ELY   This would drink deep.

CANT.   'Twould drink the cup and all.   20

ELY   But what prevention?

CANT.   The King is full of grace and fair regard.

ELY   And a true lover of the holy Church.

ACT I. SCENE I.
The first act in many ways contradicts the promises and tone of the Chorus. Canterbury praises Henry extravagantly in 1.1 but also makes clear that Henry will side with the clergy in domestic matters if they provide money for his war. Henry's questions in 1.2 on his right to wage war against France can be read as either real concern or as an attempt to make the church take responsibility for the war. In the same way, the Dauphin's insulting gift provides a chance for Henry to shine rhetorically, but it is hard to ignore the fact that he wants to absolve himself of any responsibility for the "wasteful vengeance" of war. [A.C.]
1. **self:** selfsame.—**urged:** proposed, mentioned,—not necessarily 'pressed.' 3. **Was like,** etc.: was likely (to pass), and would in fact have passed. 4. **scambling:** scrambling, turbulent. 9. **temporal lands:** estates not actually used for worship or devotion. 15. **lazars:** lepers—but used rather loosely for those afflicted with other similar diseases as well. 22. **fair regard:** kindly consideration.

CANT.   The courses of his youth promis'd it not.
            The breath no sooner left his father's body   25
            But that his wildness, mortified in him,
            Seem'd to die too. Yea, at that very moment
            Consideration like an angel came
            And whipp'd th' offending Adam out of him,
            Leaving his body as a paradise   30
            T' envelop and contain celestial spirits.
            .Never was such a sudden scholar made;
            Never came reformation in a flood
            With such a heady currance scouring faults;
            Nor never hydra-headed wilfulness   35
            So soon did lose his seat, and all at once,
            As in this king.

ELY   We are blessed in the change.

CANT.   Hear him but reason in divinity,
            And, all-admiring, with an inward wish
            You would desire the King were made a prelate.   40
            Hear him debate of commonwealth affairs,
            You would say it hath been all in all his study.
            List his discourse of war, and you shall hear
            A fearful battle rend'red you in music.
            Turn him to any cause of policy,   45
            The Gordian knot of it he will unloose,
            Familiar as his garter; that, when he speaks,
            The air, a charter'd libertine, is still,
            And the mute wonder lurketh in men's ears
            To steal his sweet and honey'd sentences;   50
            So that the art and practic part of life
            Must be the mistress to this theoric.

---

24. **The courses of his youth.** King Henry's riotous youth had been set before the Elizabethan playgoers in the First and Second Parts of Shakespeare's *Henry IV.* 26. **mortified:** killed, or brought to death's door. 29. **th' offending Adam:** original sin, the hereditary sinfulness inherited from Adam. Also called 'the old Adam,' from the biblical phrase. 34. **heady currance:** impetuous current. 35. **Hydra-headed:** the Hydra was a mythical beast killed by Hercules. Each time its head was cut off, two new ones appeared. [A.C.] 38. **divinity:** theology. 45. **policy:** statecraft, diplomacy. 46.**Gordian knot:** Legend held that anyone who could untie the knot tied by Gordius would rule all Asia. Alexander the Great cut the knot; hence the Gordian knot signifies an unexpected solution to an apparently insoluble problem. [A.C.] 47. **that:** so that. 48. **chartered:** privileged.—**libertine.** Used of all kinds of unrestraint, not exclusively in the limited modern sense. 49. **the mute wonder lurketh in men's ears:** wonder keeps men silent and makes them listen eagerly. 51–52. **the art and practic part of life,** etc.: since the King never studied any of these subjects, he must have acquired his knowledge of their 'theory' from experience in practical life. Yet that does not decrease the wonder of it all, since his pursuits were not such as to give him experience in such matters. These speeches prepare us for the great change which we are to see in Henry since he became King.

    Which is a wonder how his Grace should glean it,
    Since his addiction was to courses vain,
    His companies unletter'd, rude, and shallow,   55
    His hours fill'd up with riots, banquets, sports;
    And never noted in him any study,
    Any retirement, any sequestration
    From open haunts and popularity.

ELY   The strawberry grows underneath the nettle,   60
    And wholesome berries thrive and ripen best
    Neighbour'd by fruit of baser quality.
    And so the Prince obscur'd his contemplation
    Under the veil of wildness, which (no doubt)
    Grew like the summer grass, fastest by night,   65
    Unseen, yet crescive in his faculty.

CANT.   It must be so; for miracles are ceas'd,
    And therefore we must needs admit the means
    How things are perfected.

ELY   But, my good lord,
    How now for mitigation of this bill   70
    Urg'd by the commons? Doth his Majesty
    Incline to it, or no?

CANT.   He seems indifferent;
    Or rather swaying more upon our part
    Than cherishing th' exhibiters against us;
    For I have made an offer to his Majesty—†   75
    Upon our spiritual Convocation,
    And in regard of causes now in hand,
    Which I have open'd to his Grace at large,
    As touching France—to give a greater sum
    Than ever at one time the clergy yet   80

---

53. **glean it:** pick it up by the way. 54. **vain:** idle, empty-headed. 55. **rude:** uncultivated. 58. **sequestration:** separation. 59. **popularity:** association with the common people—almost, low company. 61. **wholesome berries,** etc. This was a common theory in gardening. 66. **crescive in his faculty:** increasing in its strength. 72. **indifferent:** impartial. 74. **cherishing th' exhibiters against us:** favoring those who make representations, or proposals, against us. 76. **Upon:** as the result of.—**spiritual Convocation:** the assembly of the spiritual, or religious, dignitaries. 77. **in regard of:** in consideration of. 78. **opened:** expounded, explained.

---

† Olivier covers up the backroom dealing of the two churchmen with physical comedy; Branagh emphasizes it by having them speak in whispers in a locked room. The BBC version shows the men kneeling in prayer before an altar, an ironic comment on their conversation. [A.C.]

Did to his predecessors part withal.

ELY   How did this offer seem receiv'd, my lord?

CANT.   With good acceptance of his Majesty;
Save that there was not time enough to hear,
As I perceiv'd his Grace would fain have done,   85
The severals and unhidden passages
Of his true titles to some certain dukedoms,
And generally to the crown and seat of France,
Deriv'd from Edward, his great-grandfather.

ELY   What was th' impediment that broke this off?   90

CANT.   The French ambassador upon that instant
Crav'd audience; and the hour I think is come
To give him hearing. Is it four o'clock?

ELY   It is.

CANT.   Then go we in to know his embassy,   95
Which I could with a ready guess declare
Before the Frenchman speak a word of it.

ELY   I'll wait upon you, and I long to hear it.   *Exeunt.*

SCENE II. London. The presence chamber in the Palace.

Enter the King, Humphrey [Duke of Gloucester], Bedford, Clarence, Warwick,
Westmoreland, *and* Exeter, [*with* Attendants].

KING   Where is my gracious Lord of Canterbury?[†]

EXE.   Not here in presence.

KING   Send for him, good uncle.

WEST.   Shall we call in th' ambassador, my liege?

KING   Not yet, my cousin. We would be resolv'd,
Before we hear him, of some things of weight,   5
That task our thoughts, concerning us and France.

---

81. **part withal:** part with. *Withal* is often so used at the end of a clause. 86. **severals:** details.—**unhidden passages:** well-known facts. 95. **embassy:** message.
SCENE II.
4. **be resolved:** have our doubts cleared up. 6. **task:** occupy, trouble.

---

† The Quarto version of the play begins here and it is worth considering why Shakespeare chose to delay presenting the title character for over 120 lines. How the king is dressed—a medieval king, a general, a modern day CEO—when he does appear will immediately influence how the audience reacts to him. [A.C.]

Enter two Bishops—[*the* Archbishop of Canterbury *and the* Bishop of Ely].

CANT.　God and his angels guard your sacred throne
　　　　And make you long become it.

KING　　　　　　　　　　　　　　Sure we thank you.
　　　　My learned lord, we pray you to proceed
　　　　And justly and religiously unfold　　　　　　　　　　　10
　　　　Why the Law Salique, that they have in France,
　　　　Or should or should not bar us in our claim.
　　　　And God forbid, my dear and faithful lord,
　　　　That you should fashion, wrest, or bow your reading,
　　　　Or nicely charge your understanding soul　　　　　　15
　　　　With opening titles miscreate whose right
　　　　Suits not in native colours with the truth;
　　　　For God doth know how many, now in health,
　　　　Shall drop their blood in approbation
　　　　Of what your reverence shall incite us to.　　　　　　20
　　　　Therefore take heed how you impawn our person,[†]
　　　　How you awake our sleeping sword of war.
　　　　We charge you in the name of God, take heed;
　　　　For never two such kingdoms did contend
　　　　Without much fall of blood, whose guiltless drops　　25
　　　　Are every one a woe, a sore complaint
　　　　'Gainst him whose wrong gives edge unto the swords
　　　　That make such waste in brief mortality.
　　　　Under this conjuration speak, my lord;
　　　　For we will hear, note, and believe in heart　　　　　30
　　　　That what you speak is in your conscience wash'd
　　　　As pure as sin with baptism.

---

9. **proceed:** i.e., taking up the explanation where it was interrupted in our previous talk (see i, 1, 90 ff.).
11. **Law Salique:** the so-called Salic Law, which settled the crown of France on male heirs only. 12. **or...
or:** either...or. 14. **your reading:** your interpretation of the law. 15. **nicely charge your understanding
soul:** be so foolish as to burden your soul (which understands the truth of the matter) with guilt. The
antithesis between *nicely* and *understanding* is quite in the formal and balanced style appropriate to the
serious speeches of the historical drama. 16. **opening:** setting forth.—**miscreate:** miscreated, unrighteously
fabricated. 19, 20. **in approbation Of:** in proving the justice of—i.e., by an appeal to the judgment of war.
29. **conjuration:** solemn adjuration.

---

† This speech is one of many places where the actor's tone of voice can make a great deal of difference.
Is Henry seriously concerned about his right or just pretending? Does he see this more as a personal
responsibility ("our sleeping sword of war") or as a political necessity ("never two such kingdoms...blood")?
[A.C.]

CANT.   Then hear me, gracious sovereign, and you peers,†
      That owe yourselves, your lives, and services
      To this imperial throne. There is no bar   35
      To make against your Highness' claim to France
      But this which they produce from Pharamond:
      '*In terram Salicam mulieres ne succedant*';
      'No woman shall succeed in Salique land.'
      Which Salique land the French unjustly gloze   40
      To be the realm of France, and Pharamond
      The founder of this law and female bar.
      Yet their own authors faithfully affirm
      That the land Salique is in Germany,
      Between the floods of Sala and of Elbe;   45
      Where Charles the Great, having subdu'd the Saxons,
      There left behind and settled certain French;
      Who, holding in disdain the German women
      For some dishonest manners of their life,
      Establish'd then this law: to wit, no female   50
      Should be inheritrix in Salique land;
      Which Salique (as I said) 'twixt Elbe and Sala
      Is at this day in Germany call'd Meisen.
      Then doth it well appear the Salique Law
      Was not devised for the realm of France;   55
      Nor did the French possess the Salique land
      Until four hundred one and twenty years
      After defunction of King Pharamond,
      Idly suppos'd the founder of this law,
      Who died within the year of our redemption   60
      Four hundred twenty-six; and Charles the Great
      Subdu'd the Saxons, and did seat the French
      Beyond the river Sala, in the year
      Eight hundred five. Besides, their writers say,
      King Pepin, which deposed Childeric,   65
      Did, as heir general, being descended
      Of Blithild, which was daughter to King Clothair,
      Make claim and title to the crown of France.
      Hugh Capet also—who usurp'd the crown

35. **imperial:** so called as reigning over more kingdoms than one. The adjective subtly forecasts the archbishop's intention to urge the King to assert his claim to France. 37. **Pharamond:** an old King of the Salian Franks. 40. **gloze:** gloss, interpret (often with a suggestion of a forced or tricky interpretation). 42. **female bar:** prohibition to women. 49. **dishonest:** dishonorable. 59. **Idly:** foolishly, without good reason.

†   Canturbury's speech is presented as a comic mess by Olivier, while Branagh presents it as serious, if confusing, business to the King and his nobles. [A.C.]

Of Charles the Duke of Lorraine, sole heir male   70
Of the true line and stock of Charles the Great—
To fine his title with some shows of truth,
Though in pure truth it was corrupt and naught,
Convey'd himself as heir to th' Lady Lingare,
Daughter to Charlemain, who was the son   75
To Lewis the Emperor, and Lewis the son
Of Charles the Great. Also King Lewis the Tenth,
Who was sole heir to the usurper Capet,
Could not keep quiet in his conscience,
Wearing the crown of France, till satisfied   80
That fair Queen Isabel, his grandmother,
Was lineal of the Lady Ermengare,
Daughter to Charles the foresaid Duke of Lorraine;
By the which marriage the line of Charles the Great
Was reunited to the crown of France.   85
So that, as clear as is the summer's sun,
King Pepin's title and Hugh Capet's claim,
King Lewis his satisfaction, all appear
To hold in right and title of the female.
So do the kings of France unto this day,   90
Howbeit they would hold up this Salique Law
To bar your Highness claiming from the female,
And rather choose to hide them in a net
Than amply to imbare their crooked titles
Usurp'd from you and your progenitors.   95

KING   May I with right and conscience make this claim?

CANT.   The sin upon my head, dread sovereign!
          For in the Book of Numbers is it writ:
          When the man dies, let the inheritance
          Descend unto the daughter. Gracious lord,   100
          Stand for your own, unwind your bloody flag,
          Look back into your mighty ancestors;
          Go, my dread lord, to your great-grandsire's tomb,
          From whom you claim; invoke his warlike spirit,
          And your great-uncle's, Edward the Black Prince,   105
          Who on the French ground play'd a tragedy,

---

72. **fine:** make beautiful. [A.C.] 74. **Conveyed himself as:** fraudulently passed himself off as. 88. **Lewis his.** A form of the genitive common in the sixteenth and seventeenth centuries, and occasionally found later. It is due to a mistaken idea that the -*es* (or '*s*) of the genitive stands for the pronoun *his*. —**appear:** are clearly seen. 93. **to hide them in a net:** to resort to a transparent subterfuge. A proverbial expression. 94. **amply to imbare:** to lay bare completely. 98. **the Book of Numbers.** Cf. *Numbers*, xxvii, 8. It was customary to seek authority for modern law and practice in special Hebrew legislation in the Old Testament.

> Making defeat on the full power of France,
> Whiles his most mighty father on a hill
> Stood smiling to behold his lion's whelp
> Forage in blood of French nobility.   110
> O noble English, that could entertain
> With half their forces the full pride of France
> And let another half stand laughing by,
> All out of work and cold for action.

ELY Awake remembrance of these valiant dead   115
> And with your puissant arm renew their feats.
> You are their heir; you sit upon their throne;
> The blood and courage that renowned them
> Runs in your veins, and my thrice-puissant liege
> Is in the very May-morn of his youth,   120
> Ripe for exploits and mighty enterprises.

EXE. Your brother kings and monarchs of the earth
> Do all expect that you should rouse yourself,
> As did the former lions of your blood.

WEST. They know your Grace hath cause and means and might;   125
> So hath your Highness. Never king of England
> Had nobles richer and more loyal subjects,
> Whose hearts have left their bodies here in England
> And lie pavilion'd in the fields of France.

CANT. O, let their bodies follow, my dear liege,   130
> With blood and sword and fire, to win your right.
> In aid whereof we of the spiritualty
> Will raise your Highness such a mighty sum
> As never did the clergy at one time
> Bring in to any of your ancestors.   135

KING We must not only arm t'invade the French,
> But lay down our proportions to defend
> Against the Scot, who will make road upon us
> With all advantages.

CANT. They of those marches, gracious sovereign,   140
> Shall be a wall sufficient to defend
> Our inland from the pilfering borderers.

---

107. **defeat:** destruction. The allusion is to the Battle of Crécy in 1346, a decisive victory for the English (cf. ii, 4, 54). 111. **entertain:** receive. 114. **for action:** for want of something to do. A common old sense of *for*. 126. **So hath your Highness.** *Hath* is the emphatic word. *Your grace* and *your highness*, as well as *your majesty*, were formerly used in addressing Kings. 129. **pavilioned:** tented, encamped. 137. **lay down our proportions:** plan our levies of troops. 138. **road:** inroad. 139. **With all advantages:** whenever he sees a good opportunity. 140. **marches:** borders. 141. **Shall:** surely will.

KING   We do not mean the coursing snatchers only,
        But fear the main intendment of the Scot,
        Who hath been still a giddy neighbour to us;   145
        For you shall read that my great-grandfather
        Never went with his forces into France
        But that the Scot on his unfurnish'd kingdom
        Came pouring like the tide into a breach,
        With ample and brim fullness of his force,   150
        Galling the gleaned land with hot assays,
        Girding with grievous siege castles and towns;
        That England, being empty of defense,
        Hath shook and trembled at th' ill neighbourhood.

CANT.   She hath been then more fear'd than harm'd, my liege;   155
        For hear her but exampled by herself:
        When all her chivalry hath been in France,
        And she a mourning widow of her nobles,
        She hath herself not only well defended
        But taken and impounded as a stray   160
        The King of Scots; whom she did send to France
        To fill King Edward's fame with prisoner kings,
        And make her chronicle as rich with praise
        As is the ooze and bottom of the sea
        With sunken wrack and sumless treasuries.   165

WEST.   But there's a saying very old and true—
            'If that you will France win,
            Then with Scotland first begin.'
        For once the eagle (England) being in prey,
        To her unguarded nest the weasel (Scot)   170
        Comes sneaking, and so sucks her princely eggs,
        Playing the mouse in absence of the cat,
        To tame and havoc more than she can eat.

EXE.   It follows then, the cat must stay at home.
        Yet that is but a crushed necessity,   175

---

144. **the main intendment of the Scot:** the purpose of the whole body of the Scottish nation. 145. **still:** always.—**giddy:** fickle, untrustworthy. 151. **Galling:** worrying. To *gall* is properly to 'excoriate,' 'knock off the skin.' It is often used figuratively by Shakespeare. —**Gleaned:** already stripped of its defenders. Cf. l. 153. Or perhaps proleptic.—**assays:** attacks, forays. 153. **defense:** defenders. 155. **feared:** frightened. 156. **hear her but exampled by herself:** listen to an example to Englishmen taken from the history of England itself. This refers to the captivity of David II. 160. **impounded as a stray.** Said contemptuously—'put into the pound,' as was done with cattle found wandering out of their owner's fields. 165. **sumless:** uncounted, incalculable. 169. **in prey:** absent in search of prey. 172. **Playing the mouse,** etc. The proverb alluded to is still in common use—'While the cat's away the mice will play.' 175. **a crushed necessity:** a forced (or strained) conclusion as to necessity. The point is that the conclusion that 'the cat must stay at home' is not the natural inference from what has been said; the natural inference is rather that which he proceeds to point to—that traps must be set for the mice.

Since we have locks to safeguard necessaries,
And pretty traps to catch the petty thieves.
While that the armed hand doth fight abroad,
Th' advised head defends itself at home;
For government, though high, and low, and lower,   180
Put into parts, doth keep in one consent,
Congreeing in a full and natural close,
Like music.

CANT.   True. Therefore doth heaven divide
The state of man in divers functions,
Setting endeavour in continual motion;   185
To which is fixed as an aim or butt
Obedience; for so work the honeybees,
Creatures that by a rule in nature teach
The act of order to a peopled kingdom.
They have a king, and officers of sorts,   190
Where some like magistrates correct at home,
Others like merchants venture trade abroad,
Others like soldiers armed in their stings
Make boot upon the summer's velvet buds,
Which pillage they with merry march bring home   195
To the tent-royal of their emperor,
Who, busied in his majesty, surveys
The singing masons building roofs of gold,
The civil citizens kneading up the honey,
The poor mechanic porters crowding in   200
Their heavy burthens at his narrow gate,
The sad-ey'd justice, with his surly hum,
Delivering o'er to executors pale
The lazy yawning drone. I this infer,
That many things having full reference   205
To one consent may work contrariously,
As many arrows loosed several ways
Come to one mark, as many ways meet in one town,

---

177. **pretty...petty.** The jingle is of course intentional. It emphasizes the light tone of the speech and expresses contempt for the Scots. 179. **advised:** considerate, wise. 181. **consent:** harmony, agreement— uniting the meaning of *consent* and *concent*. 182. **Congreeing:** agreeing together—more emphatic than *agreeing* simply.—**close.** In the musical sense. 183. **True.** Supplied from Quartos by Capell. 186. **butt:** the structure of turf to which the target was fixed in archery contests. Hence, 'end and aim,' 'limit,' etc. 189. **The act of order:** the method and operations of orderly, well-regulated society and government. 197. **busied in his majesty:** i.e., as busy in his royal office as they are in their humbler positions. 199. **civil:** well-behaved, peaceable, and orderly. 200. **mechanic.** Almost always used in Elizabethan England of humble toilers, with a suggestion of contempt or pity or condescension. 202. **sad-eyed:** serious-eyed—not 'sorrowful.' 203. **executors** (accented on the first syllable): executioners. 205–206. **having full reference To one consent:** conducing altogether to one harmonious purpose.

As many fresh streams meet in one salt sea,
As many lines close in the dial's center;   210
So may a thousand actions, once afoot,
End in one purpose, and be all well borne
Without defeat. Therefore to France, my liege.
Divide your happy England into four,
Whereof take you one quarter into France,   215
And you withal shall make all Gallia shake.
If we, with thrice such powers left at home,
Cannot defend our own doors from the dog,
Let us be worried, and our nation lose
The name of hardiness and policy.   220

KING   Call in the messengers sent from the Dauphin.
                                         [*Exeunt some Attendants.*]
Now are we well resolv'd, and by God's help
And yours, the noble sinews of our power,
France being ours, we'll bend it to our awe,†
Or break it all to pieces. Or there we'll sit,   225
Ruling in large and ample empery
O'er France and all her (almost) kingly dukedoms,
Or lay these bones in an unworthy urn,
Tombless, with no remembrance over them.
Either our history shall with full mouth   230
Speak freely of our acts, or else our grave,
Like Turkish mute, shall have a tongueless mouth,
Not worshipp'd with a waxen epitaph.

              Enter Ambassadors of France, *[attended]*.
Now are we well prepar'd to know the pleasure
Of our fair cousin Dauphin; for we hear   235
Your greeting is from him, not from the King.

AMBASSADOR   May't please your Majesty to give us leave
Freely to render what we have in charge;
Or shall we sparingly show you far off
The Dauphin's meaning, and our embassy?   240

---

210. **dial's:** a sun-dial is meant, not the dial of a clock. 211. **afoot:** under way. 212. **borne:** carried out.
213. **Without defeat:** without being thwarted in their individual operations. 216. **withal:** with *that*.
217. **powers:** forces. 220. **policy:** statecraft, statesmanship. 222. **are we well resolved:** all our doubts and
scruples are well settled. 225. **Or there:** either there. 233. **worshipped:** honoured.—**waxen.** Emphatic—
'even with an epitaph so little durable as one engraved in wax would be.' 238. **render:** report.

† Small cuts here indicate how directors shape the text to fit their interpretation. Olivier skips from
"We'll bend it to our awe" to "Or lay these bones...", emphasizing the personal heroism of Henry. Branagh
instead uses the first line of the speech, followed only with "or break it all to pieces", emphasizing the cost
of the coming war. [A.C.]

KING   We are no tyrant, but a Christian king,
Unto whose grace our passion is as subject
As are our wretches fett'red in our prisons.
Therefore with frank and with uncurbed plainness
Tell us the Dauphin's mind.

AMBASSADOR   Thus then, in few: 245
Your Highness, lately sending into France,
Did claim some certain dukedoms, in the right
Of your great predecessor, King Edward the Third.
In answer of which claim, the Prince our master
Says that you savor too much of your youth,   250
And bids you be advis'd. There's naught in France
That can be with a nimble galliard won;
You cannot revel into dukedoms there.
He therefore sends you, meeter for your spirit,
This tun of treasure; and, in lieu of this,   255
Desires you let the dukedoms that you claim
Hear no more of you. This the Dauphin speaks.

KING   What treasure, uncle?

EXE.   Tennis balls, my liege.

KING   We are glad the Dauphin is so pleasant with us.
His present and your pains we thank you for.   260
When we have match'd our rackets to these balls,
We will in France by God's grace play a set
Shall strike his father's crown into the hazard.
Tell him he hath made a match with such a wrangler
That all the courts of France will be disturb'd   265
With chases. And we understand him well,
How he comes o'er us with our wilder days,
Not measuring what use we made of them.
We never valu'd this poor seat of England,
And therefore, living hence, did give ourself   270
To barbarous license; as 'tis ever common
That men are merriest when they are from home.

---

242. **grace:** virtue, Christian self-control. 243. **fettered,** etc. The passions are thought of as here under control as much as prisoners are in their cells. 245. **few:** in brief, in short. 252. **galliard:** a lively dance. 254. **meeter for your spirit:** as being more appropriate to your disposition. 255. **in lieu of this:** in return for this. 261. **When we have matched,** etc. In what follows the King uses rather elaborately the technical language of court tennis. 263. **Shall:** which shall. The omission of the relative in the nominative is very common.—**The hazard:** again a technical tennis term. 266. **chases.** Another tennis term. 267. **comes o'er us with:** reproaches us with. 270. **living hence:** i.e., living out of England. The King means that his thoughts were ever in France, 'since our real residence was not in England—since, when we were in England, we were really *away from home,* France being our home.' 272. **from home:** away from home.

But tell the Dauphin I will keep my state,
Be like a king, and show my sail of greatness,
When I do rouse me in my throne of France.   275
For that I have laid by my majesty
And plodded like a man for working days.
But I will rise there with so full a glory
That I will dazzle all the eyes of France,
Yea, strike the Dauphin blind to look on us.   280
And tell the pleasant Prince this mock of his
Hath turn'd his balls to gunstones, and his soul
Shall stand sore charged for the wasteful vengeance
That shall fly with them; for many a thousand widows
Shall this his mock mock out of their dear husbands,   285
Mock mothers from their sons, mock castles down;
And some are yet ungotten and unborn
That shall have cause to curse the Dauphin's scorn.
But this lies all within the will of God,
To whom I do appeal, and in whose name,   290
Tell you the Dauphin, I am coming on,
To venge me as I may and to put forth
My rightful hand in a well-hallow'd cause.
So get you hence in peace. And tell the Dauphin
His jest will savour but of shallow wit   295
When thousands weep more than did laugh at it.
Convey them with safe conduct. Fare you well.

Exeunt Ambassadors.

EXE.   This was a merry message.

KING   We hope to make the sender blush at it.
        Therefore, my lords, omit no happy hour   300
        That may give furth'rance to our expedition;
        For we have now no thought in us but France,
        Save those to God, that run before our business.
        Therefore let our proportions for these wars
        Be soon collected, and all things thought upon   305
        That may with reasonable swiftness add
        More feathers to our wings; for, God before,

---

273. **keep my state:** maintain my royal dignity. 275. **When I do rouse me in my throne of France.** *Rouse* suggests the alert attitude of one who, while sitting, is yet ready at any moment to spring to his feet. 282. **gunstones.** Cannon balls were originally made of stone, not metal. 283. **charged:** burdened with guilt or responsibility.—**wasteful:** devastating. 297. **Convey them:** escort them.—**conduct:** guidance and protection. 300. **happy:** fortunate, opportune. 304. **proportions:** levies. Cf. i, 2, 137: 'Lay down our proportions to defend against the Scots.' 307. **God before:** God going before, under the guidance of God, with God's help. An old phrase, not to be confounded with 'before God.'

We'll chide this Dauphin at his father's door.
Therefore let every man now task his thought
That this fair action may on foot be brought.   *Exeunt.*

ACT TWO

Flourish. Enter Chorus.

Now all the youth of England are on fire,
And silken dalliance in the wardrobe lies.
Now thrive the armorers, and honor's thought
Reigns solely in the breast of every man.
They sell the pasture now to buy the horse,   5
Following the mirror of all Christian kings
With winged heels, as English Mercuries.
For now sits expectation in the air
And hides a sword, from hilts unto the point,
With crowns imperial, crowns, and coronets   10
Promis'd to Harry and his followers.
The French, advis'd by good intelligence
Of this most dreadful preparation,
Shake in their fear and with pale policy
Seek to divert the English purposes.   15
O England! model to thy inward greatness,
Like little body with a mighty heart,
What mightst thou do that honor would thee do,
Were all thy children kind and natural.
But see, thy fault France hath in thee found out   20

---

309. **task his thought:** tax his thought.
ACT II. PROLOGUE.
In this act, two views of Henry and the war are brought into direct conflict. The Chorus describes the followers of Henry as eager for honor and "crowns" but the audience is actually shown Pistol and company quarreling amongst themselves and viewing France as a chance to make money. The death of Falstaff, described rather than shown (just like the hanging of Bardolph), hints at the cost Henry and his subjects have already paid, and the treason of Cambridge, Scrope and Grey, while discovered and prevented, shows the uncertainty of Henry's present rule. [A.C.] 2. **silken dalliance:** social pleasure, which has been put off with the robes of silk appropriate to it. 10. **crowns imperial:** i.e., crowns worn by those who rule over more than one kingdom. 12. **advised:** informed.—**intelligence:** spies. 14. **policy:** diplomacy. 16. **Model to thy inward greatness.** This expression is by no means clear. Some have wished to read 'module,' i.e., a small thing, and to take *to* as meaning 'compared with' (a common sense). England would then be apostrophized as a little thing in comparison with the greatness of her minds, which would excellently fit the next line. 20. **thy fault.** Englishmen were regularly accused of treachery in the Middle Ages because of their frequent revolts against their Kings.

A nest of hollow bosoms, which he fills
With treacherous crowns; and three corrupted men—
One, Richard Earl of Cambridge, and the second,
Henry Lord Scroop of Masham, and the third,
Sir Thomas Grey, knight, of Northumberland—   25
Have, for the gilt of France (O guilt indeed!)
Confirm'd conspiracy with fearful France,
And by their hands this grace of kings must die,
If hell and treason hold their promises,
Ere he take ship for France, and in Southampton.   30
Linger your patience on, and well digest
Th' abuse of distance. Force a play!
The sum is paid, the traitors are agreed,
The King is set from London, and the scene
Is now transported, gentles, to Southampton.   35
There is the playhouse now, there must you sit,
And thence to France shall we convey you safe
And bring you back, charming the narrow seas
To give you gentle pass; for, if we may,
We'll not offend one stomach with our play.   40
But, till the King come forth, and not till then,
Unto Southampton do we shift our scene.   *Exit.*

SCENE I. *London. A street.*

Enter Corporal Nym *and* Lieutenant Bardolph.

BARD   Well met, Corporal Nym.

NYM   Good morrow, Lieutenant Bardolph.

---

23. **Richard Earl of Cambridge:** the younger brother of the Duke of York. His marriage to Anne Mortimer, great-granddaughter of Edward III's second son, Lionel, Duke of Clarence gave Richard's son a claim to the throne. [A.C.] 24. **Henry Lord Scroop of Masham:** The son of Sir Stephen Scroop who announces the execution of Bush, Green and the Earl of Wiltshire to Richard II (Cf *Richard II* 3.2). [A.C.] 25. **Sir Thomas Grey:** He was married to Westmoreland's daughter. [A.C.] 26. **gilt.** The pun on *gilt* and *guilt* was so common in the Elizabethan time that it may almost be called an idiom. 27. **confirmed:** made strong, sworn to. [A.C.] 28. **this grace of Kings:** this honor of Kings, this person who confers honor on the Kingly station. 31, 32. **Linger your patience on:** Let your patience hold out.—**well digest Th'abuse of distance:** accept without objection the illusion as to distance which we would have you feel. To digest a thing is to assimilate it in such a fashion that it causes no distress. 32. **Force a play!** by the violent exercise of your imagination, fill out those acts in the play which we cannot represent. 39. **pass:** passage. 40. **We'll not offend one stomach,** etc.: we'll offend nobody's taste—with a pun, of course, on seasickness. 41. **till the King come forth:** i.e., when the King comes forth. The audience is bidden to imagine the scene as shifted to Southampton when that scene comes in which the King enters, namely, the beginning of scene ii.

SCENE I.
Corporal Nym. Nym is a new character, not found in either part of *Henry IV.* His name comes from the old verb, A. S. *niman*; German, *nehman,* 'to take'; and is sufficiently appropriate to his character as a thief.

BARD   What, are Ancient Pistol and you friends yet?   3

NYM   For my part, I care not. I say little; but when time shall serve, there shall
        be smiles—but that shall be as it may. I dare not fight; but I will wink
        and hold out mine iron. It is a simple one; but what though? It will toast
        cheese, and it will endure cold as another man's sword will—and there's
        an end.

BARD   I will bestow a breakfast to make you friends, and we'll be all three sworn
        brothers to France. Let't be so, good Corporal Nym.   10

NYM   Faith, I will live so long as I may, that's the certain of it; and when I
        cannot live any longer, I will do as I may. That is my rest, that is the
        rendezvous of it.

BARD   It is certain, Corporal, that he is married to Nell Quickly, and certainly
        she did you wrong, for you were troth-plight to her.   15

NYM   I cannot tell. Things must be as they may. Men may sleep, and they may
        have their throats about them at that time, and some say knives have
        edges. It must be as it may. Though patience be a tired mare, yet she will
        plod. There must be conclusions. Well, I cannot tell.

                        Enter Pistol *and* Hostess Quickly.

BARD   Here comes Ancient Pistol and his wife. Good Corporal, be patient here.
        How now, mine host Pistol?   21

PIST.   Base tyke, call'st thou me host?
        Now by this hand I swear I scorn the term;
        Nor shall my Nell keep lodgers!

HOST.   No, by my troth, not long; for we cannot lodge and board a dozen or
        fourteen gentlewomen that live honestly by the prick of their needles but
        it will be thought we keep a bawdy house straight. [*Nym and Pistol draw.*]
        O well-a-day, Lady, if he be not drawn now! We shall see wilful adultery
        and murther committed.

---

4. **For my part,** etc. Nym's style of talking is that of the person who says less than he means, indulging in
awful threats of what he means to do.—**when time shall serve, there shall be smiles:** i.e., I will make up
my quarrel with Pistol when the proper time comes, but not before. There is also the suggestion of throat
cutting–creating new 'smiles.' 6. **what though:** what of it. 9. **sworn brothers:** brethren in arms—after
the old fashion of taking an oath to stand by each other and share good fortune and bad alike. 12. **That is
my rest:** that is my determination. A phrase from Primero, an old game at cards, in which when a person
was satisfied with the cards he held and was willing to rest his chances of winning upon them, he said, 'I
set up my rest,' that is, 'I am determined, resolved, fixed.' 13. **that is the rendezvous of it:** that is what
it all comes to, that is what it all amounts to. 14. **Nell Quickly:** that is, the hostess of the Boar's Head in
Eastcheap, Falstaff's favorite tavern. 18-19. **Though patience be a tired mare, yet she will plod:** Though
I am almost at the end of my patience, yet it will last a little longer. Still, there must be conclusions, i.e.,
the end must come sometime, and then let Pistol look out for himself. 22. **tyke:** hound. 28. **if he be not
drawn:** i.e., see if he hasn't drawn his sword.

BARD	Good Lieutenant—good Corporal—offer nothing here. 30
NYM	Pish!
PIST.	Pish for thee, Iceland dog! thou prickear'd cur of Iceland!
HOST.	Good Corporal Nym, show thy valour, and put up your sword.
NYM	Will you shog off? I would have you solus.
PIST.	'Solus,' egregrious dog? O viper vile! 35
	The 'solus' in thy most mervailous face!
	The 'solus' in thy teeth, and in thy throat,
	And in thy hateful lungs, yea, in thy maw, perdy.
	And, which is worse, within thy nasty mouth.
	I do retort the 'solus' in thy bowels; 40
	For I can take, and Pistol's cock is up,
	And flashing fire will follow.
NYM	I am not Barbason; you cannot conjure me. I have an humor to knock you indifferently well. If you grow foul with me, Pistol, I will scour you with my rapier, as I may, in fair terms. If you would walk off, I would prick your guts a little in good terms, as I may, and that's the humor of it. 46
PIST.	O braggard vile, and damned furious wight,
	The grave doth gape, and doting death is near.
	Therefore exhale!
BARD	Hear me, hear me what I say. He that strikes the first stroke, I'll run him up to the hilts, as I am a soldier. [*Draws.*] 51
PIST.	An oath of mickle might, and fury shall abate.
	[Pistol and Nym sheath their swords.]
	Give me thy fist, thy forefoot to me give.
	Thy spirits are most tall.

---

30. **offer nothing here:** i.e., don't offer to fight each other here. 31. **Pish!** Nym accompanies this interjection with some scornful gesture, such as snapping his fingers in Pistol's face. 32. **Iceland dog.** There was, and is, a kind of terrier called an Iceland terrier, with sharp ears. We may imagine that Nym, in accordance with his secretive and darkly hinting character, is represented as thin, with his hair cut short, and his ears thus appearing to stand out. 33. **show thy valour and put up your sword.** The confusion is expressed not merely by the intensity of her requests, but by their use both of the familiar *thou* and the respectful *you.* 34. **Will you shog off?** i.e., move away. In accordance with Pistol's suggestion that they should not fight in so public a place. 35. **'Solus.'** Pistol does not understand *solus* and regards it as a term of abuse. 36. **mervailous:** marvellous—an old form, used by Pistol in accordance with his habit of quoting from plays and speaking in the language of tragedy. The accent is on the second syllable. 43. **Barbason:** a fiend.— **conjure me:** drive me away, frighten me by a threat. Pistol uses many sentences of high-sounding jargon. Nym compares Pistol's bombast to the unintelligible language of conjuration. 44. **scour:** thrash. 45. **in fair terms:** in good style. 48. **doting death.** The senseless epithet *doting* is used by Pistol merely because of its alliterating with *death.* 49. **exhale:** breathe forth thy life, die. 52. **mickle:** great. Pistol is a coward, and when Bardolph makes so vigorous a demonstration he is quite ready to shake hands with Nym.

NYM I will cut thy throat one time or other in fair terms. That is the humor of
 it. 56

PIST. Couple a gorge!
 That is the word. I thee defy again.
 O hound of Crete, think'st thou my spouse to get?
 No; to the spital go, 60
 And from the powd'ring tub of infamy
 Fetch forth the lazar kite of Cressid's kind,
 Doll Tearsheet, she by name, and her espouse.
 I have, and I will hold, the quondam Quickly
 For the only she; and—*pauca*, there's enough. 65
 Go to!

Enter the Boy.

BOY Mine host Pistol, you must come to my master—and you, hostess. He
 is very sick and would to bed. Good Bardolph, put thy face between his
 sheets and do the office of a warming pan. Faith, he's very ill.

BARD Away, you rogue! 70

HOST. By my troth, he'll yield the crow a pudding one of these days. The King
 has kill'd his heart. Good husband, come home presently.

     Exit [*with Boy*].

BARD Come, shall I make you two friends? We must to France together. Why
 the devil should we keep knives to cut one another's throats?

PIST. Let floods o'erswell, and fiends for food howl on. 75

NYM You'll pay me the eight shillings I won of you at betting?

PIST. Base is the slave that pays.

NYM That now I will have. That's the humor of it.

PIST. As manhood shall compound. Push home. *They draw.*

---

54. **tall:** courageous. 57. **Couple a gorge!** Pistol has picked up a few words of French, perhaps in preparation for his foreign campaign. What he means is *couper la gorge,* 'to cut the throat.' Nym's refusal to shake hands sets Pistol off again. 59. **O hound of Crete.** Doubtless a tag from some old play. 60. **spital:** hospital. 61. **powdering tub:** a tub in which beef was powdered, i.e., salted. 62. **lazar:** leper.—**kite:** a kite was a bird of prey, of ignoble lineage, as compared with the falcon. **Cressid:** the heroine of Chaucer's poem, *Troilus and Criseyde.* She became a symbol for unfaithfulness in love, because she transferred her affections from Troilus to Diomede. The same story is worked up very cynically in Shakespeare's *Troilus and Cressida.* 65. **For the only she:** as the only woman in the world for me. *She* was used not uncommonly as a noun.—**pauca:** few words, enough said. 71. **yield the crow a pudding:** a proverbial expression for 'die'. 72. **killed his heart.** i.e., by punishing him; 'he has broken his heart,' as we would say.—**presently:** instantly. 75. **Let floods o'erswell, and fiends for food howl on!** This sounds defiant. Pistol in his turn is now disinclined to accept reconciliation. 79. **As manhood shall compound:** i.e., we will settle this debt by fighting it out like men.

BARD   By this sword, he that makes the first thrust, I'll kill him! By this sword, I will.   [*Draws.*]   81

PIST.   'Sword' is an oath, and oaths must have their course.
                                                      [*Sheathes his sword.*]

BARD   Corporal Nym, an thou wilt be friends, be friends; an thou wilt not, why then be enemies with me too. Prithee put up.

NYM   I shall have my eight shillings I won of you at betting?   85

PIST.   A noble shalt thou have, and present pay;
        And liquor likewise will I give to thee,
        And friendship shall combine, and brotherhood.
        I'll live by Nym, and Nym shall live by me.
        Is not this just? For I shall sutler be   90
        Unto the camp, and profits will accrue.
        Give me thy hand.   [*Nym sheathes his sword.*]

NYM   I shall have my noble?

PIST.   In cash, most justly paid.

NYM   Well then, that's the humour of't.   [*They shake hands.*]   95

                        Enter Hostess.

HOST.   As ever you came of women, come in quickly to Sir John. Ah, poor heart! he is so shak'd of a burning quotidian tertian that it is most lamentable to behold. Sweet men, come to him.

NYM   The King hath run bad humors on the knight; that's the even of it.

PIST.   Nym, thou hast spoke the right.   100
        His heart is fracted and corroborate.

NYM   The King is a good king, but it must be as it may. He passes some humors and careers.

PIST.   Let us condole the knight, for, lambkins, we will live.   *Exeunt.*

---

86. **A noble:** one third of a pound. Not quite the full amount of the debt, but satisfactory to Pistol because present pay—i.e., cash down—is promised. 89. **I'll live by Nym,** etc.: i.e., by means of Nym. Very likely there is a pun, whether Pistol intends it or not, since *nym* means 'to take' and Pistol expects to live by thievery. 97. **quotidian tertian.** In a quotidian ague the fit came every day; in a tertian ague, every other day. The hostess has mixed her terms, as usual. 99. **hath run bad humors on the knight:** has forced the knight to put up with disagreeable treatment. 101. **fracted:** broken.—**corroborate:** properly 'strengthen,' but misused by Pistol to mean 'broken to pieces.' 102. **He passes some humors and careers:** He makes people put up with various whims and queer courses of action. 104. **for, lambkins, we will live.** Ironic, considering that by the end of the play all the characters in this scene except Pistol will be dead. [A.C.]

SCENE II. *Southampton. A council chamber.*

Enter Exeter, Bedford, *and* Westmoreland.

BED.	Fore God, his Grace is bold to trust these traitors.
EXE.	They shall be apprehended by-and-by.
WEST.	How smooth and even they do bear themselves,
	As if allegiance in their bosoms sat,
	Crowned with faith and constant loyalty.

5

BED.	The King hath note of all that they intend,
	By interception which they dream not of.
EXE.	Nay, but the man that was his bedfellow,
	Whom he hath dull'd and cloy'd with gracious favours—
	That he should, for a foreign purse, so sell
	His sovereign's life to death and treachery!

10

Sound trumpets. Enter the King, Scroop, Cambridge, *and* Grey, [Lords, *and* Attendants].

KING	Now sits the wind fair, and we will aboard.
	My Lord of Cambridge, and my kind Lord of Masham,
	And you, my gentle knight, give me your thoughts.
	Think you not that the pow'rs we bear with us
	Will cut their passage through the force of France,
	Doing the execution and the act
	For which we have in head assembled them?

15

SCROOP	No doubt, my liege, if each man do his best.
KING	I doubt not that, since we are well persuaded
	We carry not a heart with us from hence
	That grows not in a fair consent with ours,
	Nor leave not one behind that doth not wish
	Success and conquest to attend on us.

20

CAM.	Never was monarch better fear'd and lov'd
	Than is your Majesty. There's not, I think, a subject
	That sits in heart-grief and uneasiness
	Under the sweet shade of your government.

25

SCENE II.
5. **Crowned.** The figure is that of allegiance as ruling in their natures. 6. **note:** knowledge. 8. **bedfellow:** bosom friend. 9. **dulled and cloyed.** A pair of words expressing practically the same idea, of which, however, the second is, as very commonly, more definite than the first. 15. **pow'rs:** forces. 18. **in head:** in an armed force. 22. **grows not in a fair consent:** does not act in perfect harmony with our sentiments.

GREY   True. Those that were your father's enemies
        Have steep'd their galls in honey and do serve you   30
        With hearts create of duty and of zeal.

KING   We therefore have great cause of thankfulness,
        And shall forget the office of our hand
        Sooner than quittance of desert and merit
        According to the weight and worthiness.   35

SCROOP So service shall with steeled sinews toil,
        And labor shall refresh itself with hope,
        To do your Grace incessant services.

KING   We judge no less. Uncle of Exeter,
        Enlarge the man committed yesterday   40
        That rail'd against our person. We consider
        It was excess of wine that set him on,
        And on his more advice, we pardon him.

SCROOP That's mercy, but too much security.
        Let him be punish'd, sovereign, lest example   45
        Breed (by his sufferance) more of such a kind.

KING   O, let us yet be merciful.

CAM.   So may your Highness, and yet punish too.

GREY   Sir,
        You show great mercy if you give him life   50
        After the taste of much correction.

KING   Alas, your too much love and care of me
        Are heavy orisons 'gainst this poor wretch.
        If little faults proceeding on distemper
        Shall not be wink'd at, how shall we stretch our eye   55
        When capital crimes, chew'd, swallow'd, and digested,
        Appear before us? We'll yet enlarge that man,
        Though Cambridge, Scroop, and Grey, in their dear care
        And tender preservation of our person,

---

30. **Have steeped their galls in honey:** have changed their resentment to affection. *Gall* is frequently used for resentment or the capacity for resentment. 33. **shall forget the office of our hand:** shall forget how to use our hands. The phrase is suggested by the biblical 'If I forget thee, O Jerusalem, let my right hand forget her cunning' (*Psalms*, cxxxvii, 5). 40. **Enlarge:** release.—**committed:** committed to prison. 43. **on his more advice:** now that he has had a chance to reflect. 44. **security:** carelessness. 46. **by his sufferance:** because he has been allowed to escape with impunity. 53. **orisons:** prayers. 54. **proceeding on distemper:** resulting from physical disorder—here the physical disturbance caused by drunkenness. A man is in a temper when all the four humors are properly balanced in his constitution. Any undue disturbance of this balance results in distemper, disorder of mind or body. 55. **winked at:** disregarded. *To wink* formerly meant 'to close the eyes.'—**how shall we stretch our eye:** how shall we contemplate with eyes sufficiently wide open—i.e., how shall we estimate at their proper enormity.

	Would have him punish'd. And now to our French causes.	60
	Who are the late commissioners?	
Cam.	I one, my lord.	
	Your Highness bade me ask for it today.	
Scroop	So did you me, my liege.	
Grey	And I, my royal sovereign.	65

KING   Then, Richard Earl of Cambridge, there is yours;
        There yours, Lord Scroop of Masham; and, Sir Knight,
        Grey of Northumberland, this same is yours.
        Read them, and know I know your worthiness.
        My Lord of Westmoreland, and uncle Exeter,   70
        We will aboard to-night.—Why how now, gentlemen?
        What see you in those papers that you lose
        So much complexion?—Look ye, how they change.
        Their cheeks are paper.—Why, what read you there
        That hath so cowarded and chas'd your blood   75
        Out of appearance?

CAM.   I do confess my fault,
        And do submit me to your Highness' mercy.

GREY, SCROOP   To which we all appeal.

KING   The mercy that was quick in us but late,
        By your own counsel is suppress'd and kill'd.   80
        You must not dare (for shame) to talk of mercy;
        For your own reasons turn into your bosoms
        As dogs upon their masters, worrying you.
        See you, my princes and my noble peers,
        These English monsters! My Lord of Cambridge here,   85
        You know how apt our love was to accord
        To furnish him with all appertinents
        Belonging to his honour; and this man
        Hath, for a few light crowns, lightly conspir'd
        And sworn unto the practices of France   90
        To kill us here in Hampton. To the which
        This knight, no less for bounty bound to us
        Than Cambridge is, hath likewise sworn. But O,
        What shall I say to thee, Lord Scroop, thou cruel,

61–63. **the late commissioners:** the persons lately appointed to act as a commission in England in place of the King while he is absent in France. 66. **there is yours:** i.e., your commission. The King hands to each of the traitors an order of arrest on the charge of high treason. 79. **quick:** alive. 86. **apt:** ready. Much more active in sense than in modern English. 87. **appertinents:** appurtenances. 89. **lightly:** with levity, easily, without consideration or scruple. The pun expresses contempt. 90. **practices:** plots.

Ingrateful, savage, and inhuman creature?   95
Thou that didst bear the key of all my counsels,
That knew'st the very bottom of my soul,
That (almost) mightst have coin'd me into gold,
Wouldst thou have practis'd on me for thy use—
May it be possible that foreign hire   100
Could out of thee extract one spark of evil
That might annoy my finger? 'Tis so strange
That, though the truth of it stands off as gross
As black and white, my eye will scarcely see it.
Treason and murther ever kept together,   105
As two yoke-devils sworn to either's purpose,
Working so grossly in a natural cause
That admiration did not whoop at them;
But thou ('gainst all proportion) didst bring in
Wonder to wait on treason and on murther;   110
And whatsoever cunning fiend it was
That wrought upon thee so preposterously
Hath got the voice in hell for excellence.
All other devils that suggest by treasons
Do botch and bungle up damnation   115
With patches, colors, and with forms being fetch'd
From glist'ring semblances of piety;
But he that temper'd thee bade thee stand up,
Gave thee no instance why thou shouldst do treason,
Unless to dub thee with the name of traitor.   120
If that same demon that hath gull'd thee thus
Should with his lion gait walk the whole world,
He might return to vasty Tartar back
And tell the legions, 'I can never win

103, 104. **stands off as gross As black and white:** is as plain as black is when contrasted with white. This carries on the writing motif begun when Henry reveals his knowledge to the traitors through the "papers." [A.C.] 107. **Working so grossly in a natural cause:** operating together with such obvious fitness in carrying out the purposes to which they were both inclined by nature. 108. **admiration did not whoop at them:** wonder never cried out at them. The general thought is that nobody has ever been surprised at seeing murder and treason on the part of the same person, since they are natural associates, but that now at least it is astonishing that this particular traitor, Lord Scrope, should also be a murderer. 110. **to wait on:** to accompany. 112. **preposterously:** monstrously, against nature. 113. **Hath got the voice in hell for excellence:** has won for himself the vote of all the devils as being the best of them. 114. **suggest:** tempt. 115. **botch and bungle up damnation:** patch up a crime which deserves damnation with all sorts of pretenses to make it look virtuous. 116. **colors:** often used in the sense of 'pretext.' 118. **tempered thee:** worked thee to his will, induced thee to commit this crime. *To temper* means 'to warm.' It is then often used for warming wax so that it can be moulded, and then in the sense of 'to mould,' as in this passage, figuratively.—**bade thee stand up:** abruptly ordered thee. 'Arise and go about this wicked business without affording me any pretext or excuses for so doing.' 119. **instance:** reason. 122. **with his lion gait walk the whole world.** A biblical figure. Cf. *1 Peter*, v, 8: 'Your adversary the devil, as a roaring lion, walketh about, seeking whom he may devour.' 123. **Tartar:** Tartarus, hell.

A soul so easy as that Englishman's.'   125
O, how hast thou with jealousy infected
The sweetness of affiance! Show men dutiful?
Why, so didst thou. Seem they grave and learned?
Why, so didst thou. Come they of noble family?
Why, so didst thou. Seem they religious?   130
Why, so didst thou. Or are they spare in diet,
Free from gross passion or of mirth or anger,
Constant in spirit, not swerving with the blood,
Garnish'd and deck'd in modest complement,
Not working with the eye without the ear,   135
And but in purged judgment trusting neither?
Such and so finely bolted didst thou seem;
And thus thy fall hath left a kind of blot
To mark the full-fraught man and best indu'd
With some suspicion. I will weep for thee;   140
For this revolt of thine, methinks, is like
Another fall of man. Their faults are open.
Arrest them to the answer of the law;
And God acquit them of their practices!

EXE.   I arrest thee of high treason by the name of Richard Earl   145
            of Cambridge.
        I arrest thee of high treason by the name of Henry Lord Scroop of
            Masham.
        I arrest thee of high treason by the name of Thomas Grey, knight, of
            Northumberland.   150

SCROOP Our purposes God justly hath discover'd,
        And I repent my fault more than my death,
        Which I beseech your Highness to forgive,
        Although my body pay the price of it.

---

126. **jealousy:** suspicion. 127. **affiance:** allegiance, trust.—**Show:** appear. 128. **grave:** dignified, settled in character. 133. **swerving with the blood:** turning aside at every impulse. 134. **Garnished and decked in modest complement:** furnished with every appearance of moderation and self-control. *Complement* often means 'outward appearance.' In the phrase *modest complement* the order of ideas appears to be the opposite from that in modern English. This *modest complement* means 'the complement of modesty,' that is to say, 'the appearance of modesty.' 135. **Not working with the eye without the ear:** not acting rashly on the basis of what you see without some evidence that has come by ear. 136. **but in purged judgment trusting neither:** trust neither the evidence of the eye nor that of the ear except on the basis of well-tried and clarified consideration. 137. **so finely bolted:** of so fine (literally, so thoroughly sifted) a nature. 139. **full-fraught:** full freighted—i.e., fully furnished with all good qualities.—**indued:** endowed. 142. **Another fall of man.** Note the continuation of biblical phraseology in the King's speech. 144. **God acquit them of their practices!** God forgive them for their plots. 154. **did not seduce:** Shakespeare's original audience would have recognized this as a reference to continued attempts to place the heir of Richard II (Edmund Mortimer) on the throne, and a rejection of Henry V as the legitimate king, since his father, Henry IV, usurped the throne from Richard II. [A.C.]

CAM.   For me, the gold of France did not seduce,   155
        Although I did admit it as a motive
        The sooner to effect what I intended.
        But God be thanked for prevention,
        Which I in sufferance heartily will rejoice,
        Beseeching God, and you, to pardon me.   160

GREY   Never did faithful subject more rejoice
        At the discovery of most dangerous treason
        Than I do at this hour joy o'er myself,
        Prevented from a damned enterprise.
        My fault, but not my body, pardon, sovereign.   165

KING   God quit you in his mercy! Hear your sentence.
        You have conspir'd against our royal person,
        Join'd with an enemy proclaim'd, and from his coffers
        Receiv'd the golden earnest of our death;
        Wherein you would have sold your king to slaughter,   170
        His princes and his peers to servitude,
        His subjects to oppression and contempt,
        And his whole kingdom into desolation.
        Touching our person, seek we no revenge,
        But we our kingdom's safety must so tender,   175
        Whose ruin you have sought, that to her laws
        We do deliver you. Get you therefore hence
        (Poor miserable wretches) to your death;
        The taste whereof God of his mercy give
        You patience to endure, and true repentance   180
        Of all your dear offenses! Bear them hence.
                        Exeunt [Cambridge, Scroop, and Grey, guarded].
        Now, lords, for France; the enterprise whereof
        Shall be to you as us, like glorious.
        We doubt not of a fair and lucky war,
        Since God so graciously hath brought to light   185
        This dangerous treason, lurking in our way
        To hinder our beginnings. We doubt not now
        But every rub is smoothed on our way.
        Then, forth, dear countrymen. Let us deliver
        Our puissance into the hand of God,   190

---

158. **prevention:** forestallment. In modern English any kind of hindrance may be called a *prevention*; in Elizabethan English the word was almost exclusively used for prevention by anticipation. 159. **in sufferance:** even while I am suffering death. 169. **earnest:** partial payment in advance to bind the bargain. 175. **tender:** hold, regard. 181. **dear offenses:** heinous offenses. *Dear* is used of anything that affects one nearly, whether of love or hate, joy or sorrow. 188. **rub:** impediment. A figure from bowling. 190. **puissance:** powers, forces. Trisyllabic.

Putting it straight in expedition.
Cheerly to sea; the signs of war advance.
No king of England, if not King of France!   *Flourish. Exeunt.*

Scene III. *London. Before the Boar's Head Tavern, Eastcheap.*

Enter Pistol, Nym, Bardolph, Boy, *and* Hostess.

HOST.   Prithee, honey-sweet husband, let me bring thee to Staines.

PIST.   No; for my manly heart doth ern.
Bardolph, be blithe; Nym, rouse thy vaunting veins;
Boy, bristle thy courage up; for Falstaff he is dead,
And we must ern therefore.   5

BARD   Would I were with him, wheresome'er he is, either in heaven or in hell!

HOST.†   Nay sure, he's not in hell! He's in Arthur's bosom, if ever man went to Arthur's bosom. 'A made a finer end, and went away an it had been any christom child. 'A parted ev'n just between twelve and one, ev'n at the turning o' th' tide. For after I saw him fumble with the sheets, and play with flowers, and smile upon his fingers' ends, I knew there was but one way; for his nose was as sharp as a pen, and 'a babbled of green fields. 'How now, Sir John?' quoth I. 'What, man? be o' good cheer.' So 'a cried out 'God, God, God!' three or four times. Now I, to comfort him, bid him 'a should not think of God; I hop'd there was no need to trouble himself with any such thoughts yet. So 'a bade me lay more clothes on

---

191. **in expedition.** The word implies not only expedition in the concrete sense, but also *haste.* 192. **the signs of war advance:** lift up the warlike standards. *Advance* in this sense is very common.
SCENE III.
1. **bring:** accompany, escort. 2. **ern:** grieve. 7. **Arthur's bosom.** The Hostess confuses Abraham's bosom (*Luke,* xvi, 22) with the myth of King Arthur in the earthly paradise of Avalon. 8. **'A:** an abbreviated form of *he.*—**an:** as if. 9. **christom child:** the Hostess means 'child just christened'. 10. **the turning o' th' tide:** i.e., the moment when the time changes from night to day. *Tide* often means 'time' (which is, indeed, its original sense). Many think that *tide* is here used of the sea, and it is true that there is a belief that people die at ebb-tide rather than at flood. 10.-11. **play with flowers:** pick at the bedclothes, as if he were plucking flowers.—**smile upon his fingers' ends:** Falstaff held up his fingers and smiled at them, imagining that he was looking at the flowers he had plucked. 12. **'a babbled of green fields.** It was because Falstaff talked of green fields in his delirium that the Hostess knew that he was 'playing with flowers.' Otherwise she would not have given this interpretation to his picking at the coverlet. This establishes, if any support is necessary, the correctness of Theobald's marvellous emendation of the Folio reading 'and a Table of green fields' to 'and 'a babbled of green fields,' one of the most famous cruxes in Shakespeare. Some have suggested that Falstaff was repeating bits of the Psalms,—'he maketh me to lie down in green pastures,' Theobald's reading has been almost universally accepted as restoring perhaps the most pathetic passage in all Shakespeare.

---

† The Hostess' speech is full of typical Elizabethan comedy—misused words and accidental sexual innuendo—and therefore it seems likely that it was intended to be funny. However, modern productions inevitably present it as somber and reflective. [A.C.]

his feet. I put my hand into the bed and felt them, and they were as cold as any stone. Then I felt to his knees, and so upward and upward, and all was as cold as any stone.

NYM   They say he cried out of sack.   20

HOST.   Ay, that 'a did.

BARD   And of women.

HOST.   Nay, that 'a did not.

BOY   Yes, that 'a did, and said they were devils incarnate.

HOST.   'A could never abide carnation; 'twas a colour he never lik'd.   25

BOY   'A said once the devil would have him about women.

HOST.   'A did in some sort, indeed, handle women; but then he was rheumatic, and talk'd of the Whore of Babylon.

BOY   Do you not remember 'a saw a flea stick upon Bardolph's nose, and 'a said it was a black soul burning in hellfire?   30

BARD   Well, the fuel is gone that maintain'd that fire. That's all the riches I got in his service.

NYM   Shall we shog? The King will be gone from Southampton.

PIST.   Come, let's away. My love, give me thy lips.
Look to my chattels and my moveables.   35
Let senses rule. The word is 'Pitch and pay.'
Trust none;
For oaths are straws, men's faiths are wafer-cakes,
And Hold-fast is the only dog, my duck.
Therefore *Caveto* be thy counsellor.   40
Go, clear thy crystals. Yoke-fellows in arms,
Let us to France, like horse-leeches, my boys,
To suck, to suck, the very blood to suck!

BOY   And that's but unwholesome food, they say.

PIST.   Touch her soft mouth, and march.   45

BARD   Farewell, hostess   [*Kisses her.*]

NYM   I cannot kiss, that is the humor of it; but *adieu*!

PIST.   Let housewifery appear. Keep close, I thee command.

HOST.   Farewell. *adieu*!   *Exeunt.*

---

20. **of:** on, against. 27. **handle:** discuss.—**rheumatic:** the Hostess means 'lunatic,' 'delirious.' 33. **shog:** move on. Cf. ii, 1, 47. 35. **moveables:** furniture, etc. 36. **Let senses rule:** let prudence govern (in the management of the tavern).—**Pitch:** plank down your money. 40. **Caveto:** beware, be on your guard. 41. **clear thy crystals:** wipe your eyes. 48. **Keep close:** live retired, don't go about.

SCENE IV. *France. The* French King's *Palace.*

Flourish. Enter the French King, *the* Dauphin, *the* Dukes of Berri
and Britain, [*the* Constable, *and others*].

KING   Thus comes the English with full power upon us,†
           And more than carefully it us concerns
           To answer royally in our defenses.
           Therefore the Dukes of Berri and Britain,
           Of Brabant and of Orleans, shall make forth,   5
           And you, Prince Dauphin, with all swift dispatch,
           To line and new repair our towns of war
           With men of courage and with means defendant;
           For England his approaches makes as fierce
           As waters to the sucking of a gulf.   10
           It fits us then to be as provident
           As fear may teach us out of late examples
           Left by the fatal and neglected English
           Upon our fields.

DAU.   My most redoubted father,‡
           It is most meet we arm us 'gainst the foe;   15
           For peace itself should not so dull a kingdom
           (Though war nor no known quarrel were in question)
           But that defenses, musters, preparations
           Should be maintain'd, assembled, and collected,
           As were a war in expectation.   20
           Therefore I say 'tis meet we all go forth
           To view the sick and feeble parts of France;
           And let us do it with no show of fear,
           No, with no more than if we heard that England
           Were busied with a Whitsun morris dance;   25
           For, my good liege, she is so idly king'd,

SCENE IV.
1. **power:** forces. 7. **line:** strengthen, fortify. 10. **gulf:** whirlpool, maelstrom. 13. **the fatal and neglected English:** the fatally neglected English. The *late examples* are those of Crecy and Poictiers. 14. **redoubted:** feared. 25. **Whitsun morris dance.** Whitsuntide was the time of spring festivities, among which the morris dance—a fantastic dance involving bells and hobby-horses—was conspicuous. 26. **so idly kinged:** furnished with so vain and empty-headed a king.

---

† This is the second royal court presented, and directors often make the French and their surroundings more colorful, luxurious, and more chaotic, indicating both why France is a prize worth fighting for, and why the French will lose. [A.C.]
‡ Historically, King Charles was insane, and directors often use this fact to shape their interpretation. Olivier, for example, has the French King curled up at the foot of his throne, speaking his lines mostly to himself. [A.C.]

Her scepter so fantastically borne,
By a vain, giddy, shallow, humorous youth,
That fear attends her not.

CON.   O peace, Prince Dauphin!
You are too much mistaken in this king.   30
Question your Grace the late ambassadors,
With what great state he heard their embassy,
How well supplied with noble counsellors,
How modest in exception, and withal
How terrible in constant resolution,   35
And you shall find his vanities forespent
Were but the outside of the Roman Brutus,
Covering discretion with a coat of folly;
As gardeners do with ordure hide those roots
That shall first spring and be most delicate.   40

DAU.   Well, 'tis not so, my Lord High Constable.
But though we think it so, it is no matter.
In cases of defense 'tis best to weigh
The enemy more mighty than he seems.
So the proportions of defense are fill'd;   45
Which of a weak and niggardly projection
Doth, like a miser, spoil his coat with scanting
A little cloth.

KING   Think we King Harry strong;
And, princes, look you strongly arm to meet him.
The kindred of him hath been flesh'd upon us;   50
And he is bred out of that bloody strain
That haunted us in our familiar paths.
Witness our too much memorable shame
When Cressy battle fatally was struck,
And all our princes captiv'd, by the hand   55
Of that black name, Edward, Black Prince of Wales;
Whiles that his mountain sire—on mountain standing,

---

27. **so fantastically borne:** borne by so fantastic a creature, by such a fop or buffoon. 28. **humorous:** capricious, governed by whims and impulses. 34. **How modest in exception:** how moderate, self-controlled, in taking exception, or objecting.—**withal:** at the same time. 35. **constant:** firm. 36. **his vanities forespent:** his past follies. 37. **Brutus:** Brutus the Liberator, who pretended to be an idiot in order to remain unmolested by King Tarquin. 41. **Constable:** the chief military officer of France. 46. **of a weak and niggardly projection:** if they are planned on a feeble and niggardly scale. 47. **Doth.** The subject is the idea contained in what precedes—the fact that defensive measures are weakly planned. 50. **hath been flesh'd upon us:** hath been initiated in fighting against us, or hath been made fierce by feeding upon us. 51. **strain:** race, family. 54. **Cressy battle:** Edward the Third's victory over the French in 1346.—**struck:** fought. 57. **his mountain sire:** Edward III, born among the mountains of Wales. Notice the repetition of the word.

Up in the air, crown'd with the golden sun—
Saw his heroical seed, and smil'd to see him,
Mangle the work of nature, and deface   60
The patterns that by God and by French fathers
Had twenty years been made. This is a stem
Of that victorious stock; and let us fear
The native mightiness and fate of him.

Enter a Messenger.

MESS.   Ambassadors from Harry King of England   65
        Do crave admittance to your Majesty.

KING   We'll give them present audience. Go, and bring them.

        [*Exeunt* Messenger *and certain Lords.*]

        You see this chase is hotly followed, friends.

DAU.   Turn head, and stop pursuit; for coward dogs
        Most spend their mouths when what they seem to threaten   70
        Runs far before them. Good my sovereign,
        Take up the English short, and let them know
        Of what a monarchy you are the head.
        Self-love, my liege, is not so vile a sin
        As self-neglecting.

        Enter [Lords, *with*] Exeter [*and* Train].

KING   From our brother England?   75

EXE.   From him, and thus he greets your Majesty:
        He wills you, in the name of God Almighty,
        That you divest yourself, and lay apart
        The borrowed glories that by gift of heaven,
        By law of nature and of nations, 'longs   80
        To him and to his heirs—namely, the crown
        And all wide-stretched honors that pertain
        By custom, and the ordinance of times,
        Unto the crown of France. That you may know
        'Tis no sinister nor no awkward claim,   85
        Pick'd from the wormholes of long-vanish'd days,
        Nor from the dust of old oblivion rak'd,
        He sends you this most memorable line,   [*Gives a paper.*]
        In every branch truly demonstrative;

---

67. **present:** immediate. 75. **England:** the King of England. 83. **the ordinance of times:** ancient laws—
especially the Salic Law. 85. **sinister:** literally, 'left-handed,' and so 'irregular,' with special allusion to the
bar sinister, which is used in heraldry to denote illegitimate birth.—**awkward:** literally, 'back-handed,' and
so 'indirect,' 'unlawful.' 88. **line:** pedigree. 89. **demonstrative:** proving his claim.

Willing you overlook this pedigree;   90
And when you find him evenly deriv'd
From his most fam'd of famous ancestors,
Edward the Third, he bids you then resign
Your crown and kingdom, indirectly held
From him, the native and true challenger.   95

KING   Or else what follows?

EXE.   Bloody constraint; for if you hide the crown
Even in your hearts, there will he rake for it,
Therefore in fiery tempest is he coming,
In thunder and in earthquake, like a Jove;   100
That, if requiring fail, he will compel;
And bids you, in the bowels of the Lord,
Deliver up the crown, and to take mercy
On the poor souls for whom this hungry war
Opens his vasty jaws; and on your head   105
Turns he the widows' tears, the orphans' cries,
The dead men's blood, the pining maidens' groans,
For husbands, fathers, and betrothed lovers
That shall be swallowed in this controversy.
This is his claim, his threat'ning, and my message;   110
Unless the Dauphin be in presence here,
To whom expressly I bring greeting too.

KING   For us, we will consider of this further.
Tomorrow shall you bear our full intent
Back to our brother England.

DAU.   For the Dauphin,   115
I stand here for him. What to him from England?

EXE.   Scorn and defiance, slight regard, contempt,
And anything that may not misbecome
The mighty sender, doth he prize you at.
Thus says my king: An if your father's highness   120
Do not, in grant of all demands at large,
Sweeten the bitter mock you sent his Majesty,
He'll call you to so hot an answer of it
That caves and womby vaultages of France

---

90. **overlook:** look over, examine. 91. **evenly:** in lawful and regular succession—opposed to *sinister* and *awkward* in l. 85. 94. **indirectly:** unjustly. 95. **challenger:** claimant. 101. **That:** so that.—**requiring:** request. 102. **in the bowels of the Lord:** by the compassion of the Lord. *In* is used in adjurations in the sense of 'by.' *Bowels* is a biblical word for 'mercy,' 'compassion.' 113. **For us:** for my part. 121. **at large:** in full. 124. **womby vaultages:** hollow caverns.

| | Shall chide your trespass, and return your mock | 125 |
| | In second accent of his ordinance. | |

DAU.   Say, if my father render fair return,
         It is against my will; for I desire
         Nothing but odds with England. To that end,
         As matching to his youth and vanity,   130
         I did present him with the Paris balls.

EXE.   He'll make your Paris Louvre shake for it,
         Were it the mistress court of mighty Europe;
         And be assur'd you'll find a difference,
         As we his subjects have in wonder found,   135
         Between the promise of his greener days
         And these he masters now. Now he weighs time
         Even to the utmost grain. That you shall read
         In your own losses, if he stay in France.

KING   Tomorrow shall you know our mind at full.   140

EXE.   Dispatch us with all speed, lest that our king
         Come here himself to question our delay;
         For he is footed in this land already.

KING   You shall be soon dispatch'd with fair conditions.
         A night is but small breath and little pause   145
         To answer matters of this consequence.   *Flourish. Exeunt.*

---

126. **second accent:** echo.—**ordinance:** ordnance. 129. **odds:** quarrel, controversy. 130. **vanity:** frivolity.
131. **Paris balls:** tennis balls. 133. **mistress court:** the chief court (a tennis term). 143. **footed:** landed.
145. **small breath:** small breathing space, short time for consideration.

ACT THREE

Enter Chorus.

Thus with imagin'd wing our swift scene flies,
In motion of no less celerity
Than that of thought. Suppose that you have seen
The well-appointed King at Hampton pier
Embark his royalty; and his brave fleet   5
With silken streamers the young Phœbus fanning.
Play with your fancies, and in them behold
Upon the hempen tackle shipboys climbing;
Hear the shrill whistle, which doth order give
To sounds confus'd; behold the threaden sails,   10
Borne with th' invisible and creeping wind,
Draw the huge bottoms through the furrowed sea,
Breasting the lofty surge. O, do but think
You stand upon the rivage and behold
A city on th' inconstant billows dancing;   15
For so appears this fleet majestical,
Holding due course to Harfleur. Follow, follow!
Grapple your minds to sternage of this navy,
And leave your England as dead midnight still,
Guarded with grandsires, babies, and old women,   20
Either past or not arriv'd to pitch and puissance;
For who is he whose chin is but enrich'd
With one appearing hair that will not follow
These cull'd and choice-drawn cavaliers to France?
Work, work your thoughts, and therein see a siege.   25
Behold the ordinance on their carriages,

ACT III. PROLOGUE.
This act is very much concerned with language and the shaping of reality, from the Chorus' request to the audience to "work, work your thoughts" to Henry's conquest of Harfleur through words, to Katherine's language lesson. Notice also the meeting of the four captains, representing an ideal, if argumentative, unity of the four nations of the British Islands (English, Scottish, Welsh and Irish) and the way the French conflate describing armor, writing poetry and war. [A.C.] 1. **imagined wing:** the wing of the imagination. 4. **well-appointed:** well-equipped. 5. **brave:** fine, handsome. 6. **young Phœbus:** sun god, or more generally the morning sun. [A.C.] 7. **Play with your fancies:** let your imagination act the play. 14. **rivage:** banks. The termination *-age* is collective. 20. **with:** by. 21. **puissance:** strength. 24. **choice-drawn:** drawn by choice (not by lot), select.

With fatal mouths gaping on girded Harfleur.
Suppose th' ambassador from the French comes back;
Tells Harry that the King doth offer him
Katherine his daughter, and with her to dowry   30
Some petty and unprofitable dukedoms.
The offer likes not; and the nimble gunner
With linstock now the devilish cannon touches,
                                    Alarum, and chambers go off.
And down goes all before them. Still be kind,
And eke out our performance with your mind.   *Exit.*

SCENE I. *France. Before Harfleur.*

Alarum. Enter the King, Exeter, Bedford, *and* Gloucester,
[*with* Soldiers *carrying]* scaling ladders at Harfleur.

KING   Once more unto the breach, dear friends, once more;[†]
Or close the wall up with our English dead.
In peace there's nothing so becomes a man
As modest stillness and humility;
But when the blast of war blows in our ears,   5
Then imitate the action of the tiger:
Stiffen the sinews, summon up the blood,
Disguise fair nature with hard-favour'd rage;
Then lend the eye a terrible aspect;
Let it pry through the portage of the head   10
Like the brass cannon; let the brow o'erwhelm it
As fearfully as doth a galled rock
O'erhang and jutty his confounded base,
Swill'd with the wild and wasteful ocean.
Now set the teeth and stretch the nostril wide,   15

---

32. **likes:** pleases. 33. **linstock:** the match, a bundle of combustibles on the end of a staff, with which old-fashioned cannon were set off.

SCENE I.
10. **portage:** portholes (the eyeholes). 11. **o'erwhelm:** overhang. The action described is that of collecting the eyebrows and causing them to jut out in a terrific frown or scowl. 12. **galled:** worn (by the waves). 13. **confounded:** beaten by the sea; or, perhaps, submerged, swallowed up. 14. **Swilled:** wasted.—**wasteful:** destructive, or barren.

---

†   The seige of Harfleur has been presented in a variety of ways, each chosen to match the director's overall interpretation. Olivier presents a storybook castle barely taller than the King on horseback. Branagh films the scene at night, full of explosions and fear. The BBC version does not show the town at all; only the scaling ladders used by the men. In *Renaissance Man*, the staged version of this scene (see Introduction) features hand-to-hand combat, despite the contradiction to the text, to better suit the military aspect of the film as a whole. [A.C.]

Hold hard the breath and bend up every spirit
To his full height. On, on, you noble English,
Whose blood is fet from fathers of war-proof!
Fathers that like so many Alexanders
Have in these parts from morn till even fought,   20
And sheath'd their swords for lack of argument.
Dishonor not your mothers; now attest
That those whom you call'd fathers did beget you!
Be copy now to men of grosser blood
And teach them how to war. And you, good yeomen,   25
Whose limbs were made in England, show us here
The mettle of your pasture. Let us swear
That you are worth your breeding; which I doubt not,
For there is none of you so mean and base
That hath not noble lustre in your eyes.   30
I see you stand like greyhounds in the slips,
Straining upon the start. The game's afoot.
Follow your spirit; and upon this charge
Cry 'God for Harry! England and Saint George!'
                    [*Exeunt.*] *Alarum, and chambers go off.*

SCENE II. *Before Harfleur.*

Enter Nym, Bardolph, Pistol, *and* Boy.

BARD   On, on, on, on, on! to the breach, to the breach!

NYM   Pray thee, Corporal, stay. The knocks are too hot; and, for mine own
            part, I have not a case of lives. The humor of it is too hot; that is the very
            plain-song of it.

PIST.   The plain-song is most just; for humors do abound.   5
                Knocks go and come; God's vassals drop and die;
                    And sword and shield
                    In bloody field
                    Doth win immortal fame.

16, 17. **bend up every spirit To his full height** stretch every energy to its utmost power. The figure is from
bending a bow or from winding up an engine of war (like a catapult or ballista) till it is on the stretch and
ready to be discharged. 18. **fet:** fetched, derived. 21. **argument:** subject matter; and so, something to fight
about (here practically = 'opposition'). 27. **mettle:** quality (the same word as *metal*). 31. **slips:** leashes.
SCENE II.
3. **a case of lives:** a *set* of lives—as we might say, 'nine lives like a cat.' *Case* is emphatic. 5. **plain-song:** the
simple truth. *Plain-song* in music is the simple melody without variations or the like.—**just:** correct.—
humors. Used very inexactly, in Pistol's fashion. He means that there are many 'queer things' happening.

BOY   Would I were in an alehouse in London. I would give all my fame for a
         pot of ale and safety.   11

PIST.   And I:
             If wishes would prevail with me,
             My purpose should not fail with me,
             But thither would I hie.   15

BOY   As duly, but not as truly,
             As bird doth sing on bough.

                                Enter Fluellen.

FLU.   Up to the breach, you dogs! Avaunt, you cullions!
                                            [*Drives them forward.*]

PIST.   Be merciful, great duke, to men of mould!
         Abate thy rage, abate thy manly rage,   20
         Abate thy rage, great duke!
         Good bawcock, bate thy rage! Use lenity, sweet chuck!

NYM   These be good humors. Your honor wins bad humors.
                                            Exeunt [*all but Boy*].

BOY   As young as I am, I have observ'd these three swashers. I am boy to them
         all three; but all they three, though they would serve me, could not be
         man to me; for indeed three such antics do not amount to a man. For
         Bardolph, he is white-liver'd and red-fac'd; by the means whereof 'a faces
         it out, but fights not. For Pistol, he hath a killing tongue and a quiet
         sword; by the means whereof 'a breaks words and keeps whole weapons.
         For Nym, he hath heard that men of few words are the best men, and
         therefore he scorns to say his prayers, lest 'a should be thought a coward;
         but his few bad words are match'd with as few good deeds, for 'a never
         broke any man's head but his own, and that was against a post when he
         was drunk. They will steal anything, and call it purchase. Bardolph stole
         a lute-case, bore it twelve leagues, and sold it for three halfpence. Nym
         and Bardolph are sworn brothers in filching, and in Calais they stole a

---

16. **As duly, but not as truly:** i.e., you would hasten to London *duly* (as surely), but in so doing you
would not be acting *truly* (as becomes a faithful subject). 18. **cullions:** rascals. 19. **men of mould:** men
of earth, mortal men. 22. **bawcock:** my fine cock! A term of endearment, used only to men.—**chuck.**
Another similar term, but of common gender. The absurdity of Pistol's applying these pet names to the
fiery little Welshman who is driving him into the thick of the fight is obvious. 23. **These be good humors:**
i.e., my friend Pistol has the right idea.—**wins bad humors:** i.e., acts in an unpleasant way.—With Nym
humor means anything and everything. 24. **swashers:** swash-bucklers. The Boy's speech serves to instruct
the audience as to the real character of Pistol and the rest. Such of the spectators as were not familiar
with Shakespeare's *Henry IV* might need such information. 25. **serve me:** enter into my service. 26. **man:**
servant—with a pun on the other sense of man.—**antics:** buffoons. 27. **white-livered:** cowardly.—**Faces
it out:** puts a good face on it. 29. **breaks words.** Pistol's mistakes in the use of words are notorious (cf. the
phrase *broken English*). 30. **best men:** most courageous. 33. **broke:** to 'break one's head' is to draw blood
on it—not, of course, to fracture one's skull. 34. **purchase:** booty, loot.

fire-shovel. I knew by that piece of service the men would carry coals. They would have me as familiar with men's pockets as their gloves or their hand-kerchers; which makes much against my manhood, if I should take from another's pocket to put into mine; for it is plain pocketing up of wrongs. I must leave them and seek some better service. Their villany goes against my weak stomach, and therefore I must cast it up.   *Exit.* 42

Enter Gower [*and* Fluellen].

Gow.	Captain Fluellen, you must come presently to the mines. The Duke of Gloucester would speak with you.
Flu.	To the mines? Tell you the Duke, it is not so good to come to the mines; for look you, the mines is not according to the disciplines of the war. The concavities of it is not sufficient; for look you, th' athversary, you may discuss unto the Duke, look you, is digt himself four yard under the countermines. By Cheshu, I think 'a will plow up all, if there is not better directions. 50
Gow.	The Duke of Gloucester, to whom the order of the siege is given, is altogether directed by an Irishman, a very valiant gentleman, i' faith.
Flu.	It is Captain Macmorris, is it not?
Gow.	I think it be.
Flu.	By Cheshu, he is an ass, as in the world. I will verify as much in his beard. He has no more directions in the true disciplines of the wars, look you, of the Roman disciplines, than is a puppy-dog. 57

Enter Macmorris *and* Captain Jamy.

Gow.	Here 'a comes, and the Scots captain, Captain Jamy, with him.
Flu.	Captain Jamy is a marvellous falorous gentleman, that is certain, and of great expedition and knowledge in th' aunchiant wars, upon my particular knowledge of his directions. By Cheshu, he will maintain his argument

---

37. **that piece of service:** that warlike exploit.—**carry coals:** a slang phrase for 'put up with insults or affronts.' Porters who carried coals were regarded as very low indeed; hence the contemptuous use of the phrase.' 39. **handkerchers.** This form of the word was in good use in Shakespeare's time. 40. **pocketing up of wrongs:** to bear an insult or injury without resenting it was called *pocketing it* or *putting it up.* 43. The presence of an English, a Welsh, a Scottish, and an Irish captain among the *dramatis personæ* makes the spirit of the play national in the largest sense. All English-speaking peoples in the British Isles send their fighting-men to aid the King. However, in this scene it is clear how fragile the alliance is, and how willing the different captains are to turn from their joint cause (the siege of Harfleur) to regional and personal attacks. [A.C.]—**presently:** immediately. 46. **the disciplines of the war:** the principles of military science. Fluellen's hobby is Roman military theory. 48. **discuss:** report.—**is digt himself:** has dug (in his countermining operations). 50. **directions:** management. 51. **order:** conduct, arrangement. 57. **Roman.** Emphatic. Fluellen's idea is that only the Romans knew anything about military science. 60, 61. **expedition:** Fluellen's error for 'experience.' —**upon…directions:** I say this on the basis of my personal knowledge of his management.

as well as any military man in the world in the disciplines of the pristine wars of the Romans.

JAMY   I say gud day, Captain Fluellen.

FLU.   God-den to your worship, good Captain James.   65

GOW.   How now, Captain Macmorris? Have you quit the mines? Have the pioners given o'er?

MAC.   By Chrish, law, tish ill done! The work ish give over, the trompet sound the retreat. By my hand I swear, and my father's soul, the work ish ill done! It ish give over. I would have blowed up the town, so Chrish save me la! in an hour. O, tish ill done! tish ill done! By my hand, tish ill done!   72

FLU.   Captain Macmorris, I beseech you now, will you voutsafe me, look you, a few disputations with you, as partly touching or concerning the disciplines of the war, the Roman wars? In the way of argument, look you, and friendly communication; partly to satisfy my opinion, and partly for the satisfaction, look you, of my mind—as touching the direction of the military discipline, that is the point.

JAMY   It sall be vary gud, gud feith, gud Captens bath, and I sall quit you with gud leve, as I may pick occasion. That sall I, mary.   80

MAC.   It is no time to discourse, so Chrish save me! The day is hot, and the weather, and the wars, and the King, and the Dukes. It is no time to discourse. The town is beseech'd, and the trompet call us to the breach, and we talk, and, be Chrish, do nothing. 'Tis shame for us all. So God sa' me, 'tis shame to stand still, it is shame, by my hand! and there is throats to be cut, and works to be done, and there ish nothing done, so Chrish sa' me, law!   87

JAMY   By the mess, ere theise eyes of mine take themselves to slumber, I'll de gud service, or I'll lig i' th' grund for it! ay, or go to death! And I'll pay't as valorously as I may, that sall I suerly do, that is the breff and the long. Mary, I wad full fain heard some question 'tween you tway.   91

FLU.   Captain Macmorris, I think, look you, under your correction, there is not many of your nation—

---

65. **God-den:** good e'en—i.e., good evening (the regular greeting in the afternoon). 67. **pioners:** miners.—**given o'er:** given up the work. 71. **La:** law, an interjection. Captain Macmorris's brogue is that of the Elizabethan stage Irishman. Doubtless it was as close to nature as is the case with the stage brogue today, but no closer. [A.C.] 74. **a few disputations:** a short discussion. 79. **quit you:** repay you—i.e., for the pleasure I take in hearing your debate. 80. **pick occasion:** find opportunity. 81. **It is no time to discourse.** Captain Macmorris is mortified and angry at the abandonment of the mining operations (of which he had been in charge) and is in no mood for formal discussion. 83. **beseeched:** besieged. 92. **under your correction:** a courteous phrase—you will correct me if I am mistaken.

MAC.	Of my nation? What ish my nation? Ish a villain, and a bastard, and a knave, and a rascal. What ish my nation? Who talks of my nation? 95
FLU.	Look you, if you take the matter otherwise than is meant, Captain Macmorris, peradventure I shall think you do not use me with that affability as in discretion you ought to use me, look you, being as good a man as yourself, both in the disciplines of war, and in the derivation of my birth, and in other particularities. 100
MAC.	I do not know you so good a man as myself. So Chrish save me, I will cut off your head!
GOW.	Gentlemen both, you will mistake each other.
JAMY	Ah, that's a foul fault! *A parley [sounded].*
GOW.	The town sounds a parley. 105
FLU.	Captain Macmorris, when there is more better opportunity to be required, look you, I will be so bold as to tell you I know the disciplines of war, and there is an end. *Exeunt.*

SCENE III. *Before the gates of Harfleur.*

[*Enter the* Governor *and some* Citizens *on the walls.*]
Enter King [Henry] *and all his* Train *before the gates.*

KING	How yet resolves the Governor of the town?[†]
	This is the latest parle we will admit.
	Therefore to our best mercy give yourselves,
	Or, like to men proud of destruction,
	Defy us to our worst; for, as I am a soldier, 5
	A name that in my thoughts becomes me best,
	If I begin the batt'ry once again,
	I will not leave the half-achieved Harfleur
	Till in her ashes she lie buried.
	The gates of mercy shall be all shut up, 10

---

95. **Of my nation?** Macmorris is quick to suspect that Fluellen means to cast a slur on the Irish. 96. **Look you.** Fluellen keeps his temper with difficulty and grows very formal in the process. 103. **you will mistake each other:** you insist on taking each other's words in an offensive sense when no offense is meant. 104. **that's a foul fault!** 'that's a bad error in logic' 106. **required:** Fluellen means 'found.'
SCENE III.
2. **parle:** parley, conference. 4. **proud of destruction:** proudly bent on bringing destruction upon yourselves. 8. **half-achieved:** half-won.

---

† Henry's threats before Harfleur are savage and directors often mitigate them. Olivier simply cut all but the first two lines. Branagh kept most of the speech, but his silent relief and exhaustion after the Governor's response clearly signals that the threats were only a last-ditch effort to force a surrender. The BBC version cuts some of the most brutal threats, but also cuts line 54, "Use mercy to them all." [A.C.]

And the flesh'd soldier, rough and hard of heart,
In liberty of bloody hand shall range
With conscience wide as hell, mowing like grass
Your fresh fair virgins and your flow'ring infants.
What is it then to me if impious war,   15
Array'd in flames like to the prince of fiends,
Do with his smirch'd complexion all fell feats
Enlink'd to waste and desolatlon?
What is't to me, when you yourselves are cause,
If your pure maidens fall into the hand   20
Of hot and forcing violation?
What rein can hold licentious wickedness
When down the hill he holds his fierce career?
We may as bootless spend our vain command
Upon th' enraged soldiers in their spoil   25
As send precepts to the Leviathan
To come ashore. Therefore, you men of Harfleur,
Take pity of your town and of your people
Whiles yet my soldiers are in my command,
Whiles yet the cool and temperate wind of grace   30
O'erblows the filthy and contagious clouds
Of heady murther, spoil, and villany.
If not—why, in a moment look to see
The blind and bloody soldier with foul hand
Defile the locks of your shrill-shrieking daughters;   35
Your fathers taken by the silver beards,
And their most reverend heads dash'd to the walls;
Your naked infants spitted upon pikes,
Whiles the mad mothers with their howls confus'd
Do break the clouds, as did the wives of Jewry   40
At Herod's bloody-hunting slaughtermen.
What say you? Will you yield, and this avoid?
Or, guilty in defense, be thus destroy'd?

Gov.   Our expectation hath this day an end.
         The Dauphin, whom of succours we entreated,   45
         Returns us that his powers are yet not ready
         To raise so great a siege. Therefore, dread king,
         We yield our town and lives to thy soft mercy.

---

11. **fleshed:** made fierce by carnage. 17. **fell:** cruel, savage. 18. **Enlinked to:** associated with. 30. **grace:** mercy. 31. **O'erblows:** blows away.—**filthy and contagious clouds.** Contagion was thought to reside in fogs and mists. The figure is eminently fitting, since one soldier 'catches' the spirit of riot and butchery from another, until the whole army is infected.' 32. **heady:** headstrong, impetuous. 46. **powers:** forces, troops.

Enter our gates, dispose of us and ours,
For we no longer are defensible.   50

KING   Open your gates.   [*Exit Governor.*]
                     Come, uncle Exeter,
Go you and enter Harfleur; there remain
And fortify it strongly 'gainst the French.
Use mercy to them all. For us, dear uncle,
The winter coming on, and sickness growing   55
Upon our soldiers, we will retire to Calais.
Tonight in Harfleur will we be your guest;
Tomorrow for the march are we addrest.
                                        Flourish, and enter the town.

SCENE IV. *Rouen. The* French King's *Palace.*

Enter Katherine *and* [Alice,] *an old Gentlewoman.*

KATH.   Alice, tu as esté en Angleterre, et tu parles bien le langage.†

ALICE   Un peu, madame.

KATH.   Je te prie m'enseignez; il faut que j'apprenne à parler. Comment appelez-
vous la main en Anglois?

ALICE   La main? Elle est appelée 'de *hand*.'   5

KATH.   'De *hand*.' Et les doigts?

ALICE   Les doigts? Ma foi, j'oublie les doigts; mais je me souviendrai. Les doigts?
Je pense qu'ils sont appelés 'de *fingres*'; oui, 'de *fingres*.'

KATH.   La main, 'de *hand*'; les doigts, 'de *fingres*.' Je pense que je suis le bon

---

50. **defensible:** capable of defending ourselves. 54. **For us:** as for me. 58. **addrest:** prepared, ready.
SCENE IV.
This scene introduces the feminine perspective on the war immediately after the Chorus' announcement
that the French King has offered (and Henry rejected) his daughter in marriage, as well as following on
the King's threats against the women of Harfleur. It also further complicates the issue of proper language,
raised in the conversation of the four captains, all of whom speak English, but all with different accents.
The French nobles all speak perfect English, but Katherine, a princess, only now begins to learn, realizing
that she will eventually marry an English king. It is significant that her first lesson focuses on the body.
Here the French lines are translated, except where the meaning is clear from context. [A.C.] 1-5: 'Alice, you
have been in England, and you speak the language well.' 'A little, my lady.' 'I pray you to teach me, I must
learn to speak it. What do you call the hand in English?' 'The hand? It is called 'de hand'.' [A.C.] 7-10:
'The fingers? By my faith, I forget [the word for] fingers, but I will remember. The fingers? I think they are
called 'de fingres'; yes 'de fingres'. 'The hand 'de hand'; the fingers 'de fingres.' I think I am a good student;
I have learned two words of English quickly'. The humour of the scene comes from the increasingly bad
pronunciation of common English words. [A.C.]

---

†   See Introduction for a discussion of how differently Olivier and Branagh present Katherine. [A.C.]

escolier; j'ai gagné deux mots d'Anglois vistement. Comment appelez-vous les ongles?   11

ALICE   Les ongles? Nous les appelons 'de *nails*.'

KATH.   'De *nails*.' Escoutez; dites-moi, si je parle bien: 'de *hand*, de *fingres*,' et 'de *nails*.'

ALICE   C'est bien dict, madame; il est fort bon Anglois.   15

KATH.   Dites-moi l'Anglois pour le bras.

ALICE   'De *arm*,' madame.

KATH.   Et le coude.

ALICE   'D' *elbow*.'

KATH.   'D' *elbow*.' Je m'en fais la répétition de tous les mots que vous m'avez appris dès à présent.   21

ALICE   Il est trop difficile, madame, comme je pense.

KATH.   Excusez-moi, Alice; escoutez: 'd' *hand*, de *fingres*, de *nails*, d' *arma*, de *bilbow*.'

ALICE   'D' *elbow*,' madame.   25

KATH.   O Seigneur Dieu, je m'en oublie! 'D' *elbow*,' Comment appelez-vous le col?

ALICE   'De *nick*,' madame.

KATH.   'De *nick*.' Et le menton?

ALICE   'De *chin*.'   30

KATH.   'De *sin*.' Le col, 'de *nick*'; le menton, 'de *sin*.'

ALICE   Oui. Sauf vostre honneur, en vérité, vous prononcez les mots aussi droict que les natifs d'Angleterre.

KATH.   Je ne doute point d'apprendre, par la grace de Dieu, et en peu de temps.   35

ALICE   N'avez-vous pas déjà oublié ce que je vous ai enseigné?

KATH.   Non, je réciterai à vous promptement: 'd' *hand*, de *fingres*, de *mails*'—

ALICE   'De *nails*,' madame.

13-15: Listen, tell me if I speak well, 'de hand, de fingres' and 'de nails.' 'That is well said, my lady, it is very good English.' [A.C.] 20-23: 'I am going to repeat all of the words you have taught me up to the present.' 'It is too difficult, my lady, I think.' 'Pardon me, Alice, listen.' [A.C.] 24. **bilbow**: the 'bilbo' in English was a sword or iron fetters used on prisoner's ankles. [A.C.] 26: "O Lord God, I am forgetting!" [A.C.] 31. **De nick, de sin**: Katherine's mispronunciation leads her to call the neck a small cut and the chin a religious fault. [A.C.] 32-37. 'Yes. Saving your honor you pronounce the words as well as the natives of England.' 'I have no doubt that I shall learn [English], by the grace of God, and in a short time.' 'Have you not already forgotten what I have taught you?' ' No, I shall recite it to you promptly.' [A.C.]

KATH.   'De *nails*, de *arm*, de *ilbow*.'

ALICE   Sauf vostre honneur, 'd' *elbow*.'   40

KATH.   Ainsi dis-je; 'd' *elbow*, de *nick*,' et 'de *sin*.' Comment appelez-vous le pied
          et la robe?

ALICE   'De *foot*,' madame; et 'de *coun*.'

KATH.   'De *foot* et de *coun*!' O Seigneur Dieu! ce sont mots de son mauvais,
          corruptible, gros, et impudique, et non pour les dames d'honneur d'user:
          je ne voudrois prononcer ces mots devant les seigneurs de France pour
          tout le monde. Foh! 'le *foot*' et 'le *coun*'! Néantmoins, je réciterai une
          autre fois ma leçon ensemble: 'd' *hand*, de *fingres*, de *nails*, d' *arm*, d'
          elbow, de *nick*, de *sin*, de *foot*, de *coun*.'

ALICE   Excellent, madame.   50

KATH.   C'est assez pour une fois: allons-nous à dîner.   *Exeunt.*

SCENE V. *Rouen. The Palace.*

Enter the King of France, *the* Dauphin, Bourbon,
the Constable of France, *and others.*

KING   'Tis certain he hath pass'd the river Somme.

CON.   And if he be not fought withal, my lord,
          Let us not live in France; let us quit all
          And give our vineyards to a barbarous people.

DAU.   *O Dieu vivant*! Shall a few sprays of us,   5
          The emptying of our fathers' luxury,
          Our scions, put in wild and savage stock,
          Spirt up so suddenly into the clouds
          And overlook their grafters?

BOUR.   Normans, but bastard Normans, Norman bastards!   10
          Mort de ma vie! if they march along
          Unfought withal, but I will sell my dukedom

---

41. 'What do you call the foot and the gown?' [A.C.] 44: **de foot–de coun**: Alice's mispronunciation of
the words would have made them sound like 'foutre' (slang for intercourse) and 'le con' (slang for female
genitalia). Katherine reacts with appropriate horror. [A.C.]—"O Lord God! These are words of evil sound,
corrupting, gross and immodest, and not for ladies of honour to sue. I would not pronounce these words
before the lords of France for all the world! Fie. 'Le foot' and 'le coun!' Nonetheless, I shall repeat, one
more time, my lesson all together." Katherine shows her awareness of linguistic difference by refusing to
speak the words only to French lords; she realizes that however they sound, they are proper English words.
[A.C.] 51: 'That is enough for one time. Let us go to dinner.' [A.C.]

SCENE V.
2. **withal**: with. 5. **O Dieu vivant**!: O living God–**sprays**: off-shoots. [A.C.] 6. **luxury:** lust. 11. **Mort de ma
vië**: Death of my life. 'Vie' is dissyllabic. [A.C.]

To buy a slobb'ry and a dirty farm
In that nook-shotten isle of Albion.

CON.   *Dieu de batailles*! whence have they this mettle?   15
Is not their climate foggy, raw, and dull,
On whom, as in despite, the sun looks pale,
Killing their fruit with frowns? Can sodden water,
A drench for sur-rein'd jades, their barley broth,
Decoct their cold blood to such valiant heat?   20
And shall our quick blood, spirited with wine,
Seem frosty? O, for honor of our land,
Let us not hang like roping icicles
Upon our houses' thatch, whiles a more frosty people
Sweat drops of gallant youth in our rich fields—   25
'Poor' we may call them in their native lords!

DAU.   By faith and honour,
Our madams mock at us and plainly say
Our mettle is bred out, and they will give
Their bodies to the lust of English youth   30
To new-store France with bastard warriors.

BOUR.   They bid us to the English dancing schools
And teach lavoltas high and swift corantos,
Saying our grace is only in our heels
And that we are most lofty runaways.   35

KING   Where is Montjoy the herald? Speed him hence.†
Let him greet England with our sharp defiance.
Up, princes! and, with spirit of honor edged,
More sharper than your swords, hie to the field.
Charles Delabreth, High Constable of France,   40
You Dukes of Orleans, Bourbon, and of Berri,
Alençon, Brabant, Bar, and Burgundy;

---

13. **slobbery:** muddy. 14. **nook-shotten:** shot, or pushed, off into a corner of the earth. The French nobles regard England as a remote and barbarous island.15. **Dieu de bataillës:** 'God of battles.' 'Battailles' is trisyllabic. [A.C.] 17. **as in despite:** as if despising them. 18. **sodden:** boiled. The Constable refers to the national English beverage—ale. 19. **drench:** drink.—**sur-reined:** over-reined, exhausted by hard riding.— **jades:** a contemptuous term for 'horses.' Ale was often given to tired horses to refresh them. 20. **Decoct:** warm. 23. **roping:** hanging down like ropes. 26. 'Poor,' etc. *Poor* is used to correct *rich*—our fields are rich in themselves, but they are poor with regard to the character of their owners. 29. **bred out:** exhausted by in-breeding. 32. **bid us to:** bid us go to. 33. **lavoltas:** dances in which there was much jumping about.—**corantos:** dances in which there was much rapid movement over the floor. 34. **grace:** excellence. 35. **lofty:** showy, high-mannered. There is a slight pause before *runaways*. 36. **Montjoy:** the official title of the chief herald of France.

---

†   The King's character is illuminated by his reactions here. Is he finally spurred to action by the threat to his nation or the idea that Frenchwomen might prefer English lovers? [A.C.]

          Jaques Chatillon, Rambures, Vaudemont,
          Beaumont, Grandpré, Roussi, and Fauconberg,
          Foix, Lestrale, Bouciqualt, and Charolois,   45
          High dukes, great princes, barons, lords, and knights,
          For your great seats now quit you of great shames.
          Bar Harry England, that sweeps through our land
          With pennons painted in the blood of Harfleur.
          Rush on his host as doth the melted snow   50
          Upon the valleys whose low vassal seat
          The Alps doth spit and void his rheum upon.
          Go down upon him—you have power enough—
          And in a captive chariot into Rouen
          Bring him our prisoner.

CON.   This becomes the great.   55
          Sorry am I his numbers are so few,
          His soldiers sick and famish'd in their march;
          For I am sure, when he shall see our army,
          He'll drop his heart into the sink of fear
          And, for achievement, offer us his ransom.   60

KING   Therefore, Lord Constable, haste on Montjoy,
          And let him say to England that we send
          To know what willing ransom he will give.
          Prince Dauphin, you shall stay with us in Rouen.

DAU.   Not so, I do beseech your Majesty.   65

KING   Be patient, for you shall remain with us.
          Now forth, Lord Constable and princes all,
          And quickly bring us word of England's fall.   *Exeunt.*

---

47. **seats:** fiefs—in return for which they were bound to fight for the King .—**quit you of:** redeem yourselves from. 53. **power:** forces. 59. **sink:** cesspool. 60. **for achievement,** etc.: instead of winning anything from us, will offer us ransom to allow him to go home. For *achieve* = 'get,' 'obtain,' cf. iii, 3, 8: 'the half-achieved Harfleur'; and iv, 3, 91: 'Bid them achieve me, and then sell my bones.' 64. **you shall stay with us in Rouen**: The Folio has the Dauphin present at Agincourt, which appears to contradict the King's insistence here. It is impossible to say now whether this indicates Shakespeare's first plan for the Dauphin, later changed, or not. However, it fits well with both the French king's wavering and the Dauphin's habit of acting on his own to have him disobey his father's stated wishes. It is worth considering how Act IV would be different if the Dauphin was not present. [A.C.]

SCENE VI. *The English camp in Picardy.*

Enter Captains, *English and Welsh*—Gower *and* Fluellen.

GOW.   How now, Captain Fluellen? Come you from the bridge?

FLU.   I assure you there is very excellent services committed at the bridge.

GOW.   Is the Duke of Exeter safe?   3

FLU.   The Duke of Exeter is as magnanimous as Agamemnon, and a man that I
          love and honour with my soul, and my heart, and my duty, and my live,
          and my living, and my uttermost power. He is not—God be praised and
          plessed!—any hurt in the world, but keeps the pridge most valiantly, with
          excellent discipline. There is an aunchient lieutenant there at the pridge, I
          think in my very conscience he is as valiant a man as Mark Anthony, and
          he is a man of no estimation in the world, but I did see him do as gallant
          service.   11

GOW.   What do you call him?

FLU.   He is call'd Aunchient Pistol.

GOW.   I know him not.

Enter Pistol.

FLU.   Here is the man.   15

PIST.   Captain, I thee beseech to do me favours.
          The Duke of Exeter doth love thee well.

FLU.   Ay, I praise God; and I have merited some love at his hands.

PIST.   Bardolph, a soldier firm and sound of heart,
          And of buxom valour, hath by cruel fate,   20
          And giddy Fortune's furious fickle wheel,
          That goddess blind,
          That stands upon the rolling restless stone—

FLU.   By your patience, Aunchient Pistol. Fortune is painted plind, with a
          muffler afore her eyes, to signify to you that Fortune is plind; and she is
          painted also with a wheel, to signify to you, which is the moral of it, that

---

SCENE VI.
2. **committed:** Fluellen's mistake for *performed.* 4. **magnanimous:** great-souled, valiant. 8. **discipline:** military science. Fluellen's fondness for military science and for the ancients appears on every occasion. 10. **estimation:** reputation. 20. **buxom.** Perhaps Pistol means 'sturdy.' 21. **Fortune's...wheel,** etc. Pistol has combined, in a deliciously inconsistent fashion, two conceptions of Fortune. In one of these her mutability is figured by a wheel (on which she sometimes rides, as in Dürer's picture, and by which she sometimes sits and keeps it turning); in another she stands upon a rolling stone. 25. **By your patience,** etc. Fluellen cannot resist the temptation to read Pistol a little lecture on the emblems of Fortune. He is not worried by the inconsistency of Pistol's combination.

she is turning and inconstant, and mutability, and variation; and her foot, look you, is fixed upon a spherical stone, which rolls, and rolls, and rolls. In good truth, the poet makes a most excellent description of it. Fortune is an excellent moral.   30

PIST.   Fortune is Bardolph's foe, and frowns on him;
For he hath stol'n a pax, and hanged must 'a be,
A damned death!
Let gallows gape for dog; let man go free,
And let not hemp his windpipe suffocate.   35
But Exeter hath given the doom of death
For pax of little price.
Therefore, go speak—the Duke will hear thy voice—
And let not Bardolph's vital thread be cut
With edge of penny cord and vile reproach.   40
Speak, Captain, for his life, and I will thee requite.

FLU.   Aunchient Pistol, I do partly understand your meaning.

PIST.   Why then, rejoice therefore!

FLU.   Certainly, aunchient, it is not a thing to rejoice at; for if, look you, he were my brother, I would desire the Duke to use his good pleasure and put him to execution; for discipline ought to be used.   46

PIST.   Die and be damn'd! and figo for thy friendship!

FLU.   It is well.

PIST.   The fig of Spain!   *Exit.*

FLU.   Very good.   50

GOW.   Why, this is an arrant counterfeit rascal. I remember him now—a bawd, a cutpurse.

FLU.   I'll assure you, 'a utt'red as prave words at the pridge as you shall see in a summer's day. But it is very well. What he has spoke to me, that is well, I warrant you, when time is serve.   55

GOW.   Why, 'tis a gull, a fool, a rogue, that now and then goes to the wars to grace himself, at his return into London, under the form of a soldier. And

---

32. **pax:** a little tablet, containing a relic, or a picture of Christ, the Virgin, or a saint. The pax was kissed by the priest at the mass, and then was passed about to be kissed by the worshippers. Hence its name—from 'the kiss of *peace.*' 37. **little price:** small value. 41. **Speak.** The Alexandrine, proper to the old style of tragedy, is appropriate in Pistol's dialect. 42. **partly.** Fluellen finds Pistol's strange English not altogether intelligible. 43. **rejoice therefore.** Addressed by Pistol to himself. He takes Fluellen's words as implying a favourable answer. There is a comic ambiguity in Pistol's exclamation, however, as if he were congratulating Fluellen on being able to understand him at all. 47. **figo:** a fig! As Pistol says this, he makes an insulting gesture, known as 'making the fig.' 51. **bawd:** pander. 53. **prave:** brave—i.e., fine. 55. **is serve:** Fluellen's mistake for 'shall serve.' 56. **gull:** properly, dupe; but often used for 'foolish fellow' in general.

such fellows are perfect in the great commanders' names, and they will learn you by rote where services were done—at such and such a sconce, at such a breach, at such a convoy; who came off bravely, who was shot, who disgrac'd, what terms the enemy stood on; and this they con perfectly in the phrase of war, which they trick up with new-tuned oaths; and what a beard of the General's cut and a horrid suit of the camp will do among foaming bottles and ale-wash'd wits is wonderful to be thought on. But you must learn to know such slanders of the age, or else you may be marvellously mistook.   66

FLU.   I tell you what, Captain Gower, I do perceive he is not the man that he would gladly make show to the world he is. If I find a hole in his coat, I will tell him my mind. [*Drum within.*] Hark you, the King is coming, and I must speak with him from the pridge.   70

Drum and colours. Enter the King *and his poor* Soldiers, [*and* Gloucester].

God pless your Majesty!

KING   How now, Fluellen? Cam'st thou from the bridge?

FLU.   Ay, so please your Majesty. The Duke of Exeter has very gallantly maintain'd the pridge; the French is gone off, look you, and there is gallant and most prave passages. Marry, th' athversary was have possession of the pridge, but he is enforced to retire, and the Duke of Exeter is master of the pridge. I can tell your Majesty, the Duke is a prave man.   77

KING   What men have you lost, Fluellen?

FLU.   The perdition of th' athversary hath been very great, reasonable great. Marry, for my part, I think the Duke hath lost never a man but one that is like to be executed for robbing a church—one Bardolph, if your Majesty know the man. His face is all bubukles and whelks, and knobs, and flames o' fire, and his lips blows at his nose, and it is like a coal of fire, sometimes plue and sometimes red; but his nose is executed, and his fire's out.   85

---

59. **learn:** teach.—**sconce:** breastwork. 60. **convoy:** the guarding of a provision train.—**bravely:** with credit. 61. **stood on:** insisted on 62. **new-tuned:** novel-sounding. The figure comes, of course, from the affectation of knowing all the latest and most fashionable songs. 65. **slanders of the age:** persons who are a disgrace to the times. 66. **mistook.** As Fluellen has been in the present case by taking Pistol for a brave soldier. 68. **hole in his coat:** something discreditable in his record. 69. **my mind:** what I think of him. 70. **speak…pridge:** tell him the news I have brought from the bridge; or, perhaps, speak *concerning* the bridge. 75. **passages:** acts, deeds. 79. **perdition:** loss.—**reasonable.** Fluellen uses this word as if it were stronger than *very,* as of course it is not. 82. **bubukles:** carbuncles.

KING[†]   We would have all such offenders so cut off. And we give express charge
that in our marches through the country there be nothing compell'd from
the villages, nothing taken but paid for; none of the French upbraided
or abused in disdainful language; for when lenity and cruelty play for a
kingdom, the gentler gamester is the soonest winner.   90

Tucket. Enter Montjoy.

MONT.   You know me by my habit.

KING   Well then, I know thee. What shall I know of thee?

MONT.   My master's mind.

KING   Unfold it.   94

MONT.   Thus says my king—Say thou to Harry of England: Though we seem'd
dead, we did but sleep. Advantage is a better soldier than rashness. Tell
him we could have rebuk'd him at Harfleur, but that we thought not
good to bruise an injury till it were full ripe. Now we speak upon our cue,
and our voice is imperial. England shall repent his folly, see his weakness,
and admire our sufferance. Bid him therefore consider of his ransom,
which must proportion the losses we have borne, the subjects we have
lost, the disgrace we have digested; which in weight to re-answer, his
pettiness would bow under. For our losses, his exchequer is too poor; for
th' effusion of our blood, the muster of his kingdom too faint a number;
and for our disgrace, his own person kneeling at our feet but a weak and
worthless satisfaction. To this add defiance; and tell him for conclusion,
he hath betrayed his followers, whose condemnation is pronounc'd. So
far my king and master; so much my office.

KING   What is thy name? I know thy quality.

MONT.   Montjoy.   110

KING   Thou dost thy office fairly. Turn thee back,

---

86. **We would,** etc. The King 's ignoring of his former familiarity with Bardolph is grim testimony to
his reformation. 90. **Tucket:** a trumpet flourish. 91. **habit:** i.e., his herald's attire. 92. **of:** from. 96.
Advantage: caution (a considerate waiting for an advantageous opportunity). 98. **bruise:** squeeze. The
figure is from the treatment of a boil or the like.—**upon our cue:** i.e., now the proper moment has come
for us to speak. A common theatrical figure. 100. **admire our sufferance:** wonder at my patience. 102.
digested: put up with.—**in weight to re-answer:** to make full compensation for. Note that *compensate*
means literally 'to *weigh* with.' 104. **the muster of his kingdom:** the whole population of England. *Muster*
is practically equivalent to 'census.' 109. **quality:** rank and profession (as chief herald of France). 111.
fairly: handsomely.

---

†   This speech is another moment when the King's character is revealed, and can be played in a variety
of ways. How does he react to the death of one of his old friends? Olivier cuts the hanging of Bardolph
entirely. The BBC version has Henry, tearful, using the speech to reassure himself as to the rightness of
his decision. Branagh goes the furthest and has Bardolph actually hanged on screen, as Henry watches,
stricken. [A.C.]

And tell thy king I do not seek him now,
But could be willing to march on to Calais
Without impeachment: for, to say the sooth,
Though 'tis no wisdom to confess so much   115
Unto an enemy of craft and vantage,
My people are with sickness much enfeebled,
My numbers lessen'd, and those few I have,
Almost no better than so many French;
Who when they were in health, I tell thee, herald,   120
I thought upon one pair of English legs
Did march three Frenchmen. Yet forgive me, God,
That I do brag thus. This your air of France
Hath blown that vice in me. I must repent.
Go therefore tell thy master here I am;   125
My ransom is this frail and worthless trunk;
My army but a weak and sickly guard;
Yet, God before, tell him we will come on,
Though France himself and such another neighbour
Stand in our way. There's for thy labor, Montjoy.   [*Gives a purse.*] 130
Go bid thy master well advise himself:
If we may pass, we will; if we be hind'red,
We shall your tawny ground with your red blood
Discolor; and so, Montjoy, fare you well.
The sum of all our answer is but this: 135
We would not seek a battle, as we are,
Nor, as we are, we say we will not shun it.
So tell your master.

MONT.   I shall deliver so. Thanks to your Highness.   [*Exit.*]

GLOUC.   I hope they will not come upon us now.   140

KING   We are in God's hand, brother, not in theirs.
         March to the bridge. It now draws toward night.
         Beyond the river we'll encamp ourselves,
         And on tomorrow bid them march away.   *Exeunt.*

---

114. **impeachment:** hindrance. 116. **an enemy of craft and vantage:** a crafty enemy who is stronger than one's self. 124. **in:** into. 126. **trunk:** the only ransom he will offer is his own body, which the French king may have *if he can get it.* 130. **There's for thy labor.** He gives the herald a purse or a jewel. 144. **bid them march away:** give orders to our army to march towards Calais.

SCENE VII. *The French camp, near Agincourt.*

Enter the Constable of France, *the* Lord Rambures,
Orleans, Dauphin, *with others.*

CON. Tut! I have the best armor of the world. Would it were day![†]

ORL. You have an excellent armor; but let my horse have his due.

CON. It is the best horse of Europe.

ORL. Will it never be morning?

DAU. My Lord of Orleans, and my Lord High Constable, you talk of horse and armor?   6

ORL. You are as well provided of both as any prince in the world.

DAU. What a long night is this! I will not change my horse with any that treads but on four pasterns. *Ça, ha!* he bounds from the earth, as if his entrails were hairs; *le cheval volant,* the Pegasus, *avec les narines de feu!* When I bestride him, I soar, I am a hawk. He trots the air. The earth sings when he touches it. The basest horn of his hoof is more musical than the pipe of Hermes.   13

ORL. He's of the colour of the nutmeg.

DAU. And of the heat of the ginger. It is a beast for Perseus: he is pure air and fire; and the dull elements of earth and water never appear in him, but only in patient stillness while his rider mounts him. He is indeed a horse, and all other jades you may call beasts.

CON. Indeed, my lord, it is a most absolute and excellent horse.

DAU. It is the prince of palfreys. His neigh is like the bidding of a monarch, and his countenance enforces homage.   21

ORL. No more, cousin.

DAU. Nay, the man hath no wit that cannot, from the rising of the lark to the lodging of the lamb, vary deserved praise on my palfrey. It is a theme as fluent as the sea. Turn the sands into eloquent tongues, and my horse is argument for them all. 'Tis a subject for a sovereign to reason on, and for

---

SCENE VII.
This frivolous scene is in accordance with what history tells us of the demeanor of the French on the eve of the battle. 9-10. **pasterns:** the pastern is part of a horse's foot between the fetlock and the hoof.—**as if his entrails were hairs:** as if he weighed nothing, or, as if he were a tennis ball, stuffed with hair.—**le cheval volant:** the flying horse.—**avec les narines de feu:** with fiery nostrils. [A.C.] 12. **basest horn of his hoof:** the lowest note which his horny hoof sounds as it strikes the earth. 15. **Perseus:** who rode through the air on Pegasus. 19. **absolute:** perfect. 22. **No more.** Orleans is bored by the Dauphin's extravagant boasting. 24. **vary deserved praise:** utter praise in many variations, all of it well-deserved. 26. **argument:** subject.—**reason:** discourse.

a sovereign's sovereign to ride on; and for the world, familiar to us and unknown, to lay apart their particular functions and wonder at him. I once writ a sonnet in his praise and began thus, 'Wonder of nature!'

ORL.   I have heard a sonnet begin so to one's mistress.   30

DAU.   Then did they imitate that which I compos'd to my courser, for my horse is my mistress.

ORL.   Your mistress bears well.

DAU.   Me well, which is the prescript praise and perfection of a good and particular mistress.   35

CON.   Nay, for methought yesterday your mistress shrewdly shook your back.

DAU.   So perhaps did yours.

CON.   Mine was not bridled.

DAU.   O, then belike she was old and gentle, and you rode like a kern of Ireland, your French hose off, and in your strait strossers.   40

CON.   You have good judgment in horsemanship.

DAU.   Be warn'd by me then. They that ride so, and ride not warily, fall into foul bogs. I had rather have my horse to my mistress.

CON.   I had as lief have my mistress a jade.

DAU.   I tell thee, Constable, my mistress wears his own hair.   45

CON.   I could make as true a boast as that, if I had a sow to my mistress.

DAU.   'Le chien est retourné à son propre vomissement, et la truie lavée au bourbier.' Thou mak'st use of anything.

CON.   Yet do I not use my horse for my mistress, or any such proverb so little kin to the purpose.   50

RAM.   My Lord Constable, the armor that I saw in your tent tonight—are those stars or suns upon it?

CON.   Stars, my lord.

DAU.   Some of them will fall tomorrow, I hope.

CON.   And yet my sky shall not want.   55

---

34. **prescript:** special and appropriate. [A.C.] 35. **particular:** who is one's very own. 39. **kern:** peasant; more generally, one who has never been on a horse. 47-48. **Le chien,** etc. Cf. *2 Peter,* ii, 29: 'The dog is turned to his own vomit again; and the sow that was washed to her wallowing in the mire.' 55. **my sky.** There will still be stars enough in the sky of his *honor.*

---

†   Most productions do present the French as confident and at ease, but the BBC version shows them as nervous, and concealing their fear by false bragging. [A.C.]

DAU.	That may be, for you bear a many superfluously, and 'twere more honor some were away.
CON.	Ev'n as your horse bears your praises, who would trot as well, were some of your brags dismounted.
DAU.	Would I were able to load him with his desert. Will it never be day? I will trot tomorrow a mile, and my way shall be paved with English faces.
CON.	I will not say so, for fear I should be fac'd out of my way, but I would it were morning, for I would fain be about the ears of the English.
RAM.	Who will go to hazard with me for twenty prisoners?
CON.	You must first go yourself to hazard ere you have them. 65
DAU.	'Tis midnight; I'll go arm myself. *Exit.*
ORL.	The Dauphin longs for morning.
RAM.	He longs to eat the English.
CON.	I think he will eat all he kills.
ORL.	By the white hand of my lady, he's a gallant prince. 70
CON.	Swear by her foot, that she may tread out the oath.
ORL.	He is simply the most active gentleman of France.
CON.	Doing is activity, and he will still be doing.
ORL.	He never did harm, that I heard of.
CON.	Nor will do none tomorrow. He will keep that good name still. 75
ORL.	I know him to be valiant.
CON.	I was told that by one that knows him better than you.
ORL.	What's he?
CON.	Marry, he told me so himself, and he said he car'd not who knew it.
ORL.	He needs not; it is no hidden virtue in him. 80
CON.	By my faith, sir, but it is. Never anybody saw it but his lackey. 'Tis a hooded valor, and when it appears, it will bate.

---

56. **'twere more honor:** i.e., your armor is too new; you have never had any of the spangles on it knocked off in battle. 62. **faced out of my way:** browbeaten so as to abandon my course. An obvious pun. 64. **go to hazard...for twenty prisoners:** play at hazard (a game at dice) with twenty English prisoners as the stake. 71. **tread out the oath:** the idea is that the lady may fulfil the oath by dancing, since the Dauphin is more likely to distinguish himself in that way than in the battle. 82. **hooded...bate.** Falconing terms. The falcon was often carried with a hood over its head; and when this was removed, the bird was likely to *bate,* i.e., 'to flap the wings' (French *battre*). *Bate* also means 'to abate,' and in that sense is applied to the Dauphin's valor, which is likely to diminish when the time to show it actually comes.

ORL.   Ill will never said well.

CON.   I will cap that proverb with 'There is flattery in friendship.'

ORL.   And I will take up that with 'Give the devil his due.'   85

CON.   Well plac'd! There stands your friend for the devil. Have at the very eye of
that proverb with 'A pox of the devil!'

ORL.   You are the better at proverbs, by how much 'a fool's bolt is soon shot.'

CON.   You have shot over.

ORL.   'Tis not the first time you were overshot.   90

Enter a Messenger.

MESS.   My Lord High Constable, the English lie within fifteen hundred paces of
your tents.

CON.   Who hath measur'd the ground?

MESS.   The Lord Grandpré.

CON.   A valiant and most expert gentleman. Would it were day! Alas, poor
Harry of England! He longs not for the dawning, as we do.   96

ORL.   What a wretched and peevish fellow is this King of England, to mope
with his fatbrain'd followers so far out of his knowledge.

CON.   If the English had any apprehension, they would run away.

ORL.   That they lack; for if their heads had any intellectual armor, they could
never wear such heavy headpieces.   101

RAM.   That island of England breeds very valiant creatures. Their mastiffs are of
unmatchable courage.[†]

ORL.   Foolish curs, that run winking into the mouth of a Russian bear and have
their heads crush'd like rotten apples. You may as well say that's a valiant
flea that dare eat his breakfast on the lip of a lion.   105

---

83. **Ill will,** etc. The rest of this conversation is an example of the common diversion of 'capping proverbs,'—answering one proverb by another,—the person who has the last word being the winner. 97. **peevish:** childish, foolish.—**to mope:** to come blundering along, like a man walking in his sleep. 98. **fatbrain'd:** stupid.—**so far out of his knowledge:** so far away from any region with which he is acquainted. Orleans's comparison is that of a stupid fellow who blunders into a strange region and loses his way. 99. **apprehension:** common sense—not fear. The idea is that they are too stupid to know the danger they are in. 104. **winking:** with their eyes shut—i.e., with blind and stupid courage.

---

†   The first sentence of this speech is the final moment of Branagh's shaping of the character of Montjoy. By combining the parts of all French ambassadors and messengers into one, Branagh presents one character who interacts with Henry over and over, and gradually comes to admire him more than his own countrymen. Rather than another insult, this line becomes a rebuke to the arrogant French. [A.C.]

CON.   Just, just. And the men do sympathize with the mastiffs in robustious and
       rough coming on, leaving their wits with their wives, and then give them
       great meals of beef and iron and steel, they will eat like wolves and fight
       like devils.

ORL.   Ay, but these English are shrowdly out of beef.   110

CON.   Then shall we find tomorrow they have only stomachs to eat and none to
       fight. Now is it time to arm. Come, shall we about it?

ORL.   It is now two o'clock; but let me see—by ten
       We shall have each a hundred Englishmen.   *Exeunt.*

ACT FOUR

Chorus.

Now entertain conjecture of a time
When creeping murmur and the poring dark
Fills the wide vessel of the universe.
From camp to camp, through the foul womb of night,
The hum of either army stilly sounds,   5
That the fix'd sentinels almost receive
The secret whispers of each other's watch.
Fire answers fire, and through their paly flames
Each battle sees the other's umber'd face.
Steed threatens steed, in high and boastful neighs   10
Piercing the night's dull ear; and from the tents
The armorers accomplishing the knights,
With busy hammers closing rivets up,
Give dreadful note of preparation.

---

107. **do sympathize with:** resemble, are like. *Sympathy* is often used of agreement or correspondence.
[A.C.]—**robustious:** boisterous. 108. **coming on:** making an attack on, assault. 111. **shrowdly:** deucedly.
112. **stomachs to eat and none to fight.** A common pun.

ACT IV. PROLOGUE.
Although almost all productions of the play feature extended battle sequences, it is important to realize
that Shakespeare chose not to feature actual fighting here. That he could have is clear from *Henry IV, part
1*, when Prince Hal gallantly rescues his father, the king, from certain death, and engages in a chivalric duel
to the death with his foil, Hotspur. Here, in contrast, Shakespeare offers the fears of both king and soldiers
before battle, boys killed "against the law of arms" and Pistol taking one terrified French solider hostage.
1. **entertain conjecture:** receive into your minds an idea. The phrase is practically equivalent to 'imagine.'
[A.C.] 2. **poring dark.** The epithet *poring* is transferred from the person to the thing. The *poring dark* is the
dark which makes anybody pore, or look closely, in order to see anything. 4. **foul.** Because black. 6. **That:**
so that. 9. **battle:** host.—**umbered:** brown or yellowish—on account of the play of firelight on their faces.
12. **accomplishing:** finishing—i:e., putting the finishing touches to their armor.

The country cocks do crow, the clocks do toll   15
And the third hour of drowsy morning name.
Proud of their numbers and secure in soul,
The confident and over-lusty French
Do the low-rated English play at dice,
And chide the cripple tardy-gaited night   20
Who like a foul and ugly witch doth limp
So tediously away. The poor condemned English,
Like sacrifices, by their watchful fires
Sit patiently and inly ruminate
The morning's danger; and their gesture sad,   25
Investing lank-lean cheeks and war-worn coats,
Presenteth them unto the gazing moon
So many horrid ghosts. O, now, who will behold
The royal captain of this ruin'd band
Walking from watch to watch, from tent to tent,   30
Let him cry 'Praise and glory on his head.'
For forth he goes and visits all his host,
Bids them good morrow with a modest smile
And calls them brothers, friends, and countrymen.
Upon his royal face there is no note   35
How dread an army hath enrounded him;
Nor doth he dedicate one jot of color
Unto the weary and all-watched night,
But freshly looks, and overbears attaint
With cheerful semblance and sweet majesty;   40
That every wretch, pining and pale before,
Beholding him, plucks comfort from his looks.
A largess universal, like the sun,
His liberal eye doth give to every one,
Thawing cold fear. Then, mean and gentle all,   45
Behold, as may unworthiness define,
A little touch of Harry in the night.
And so our scene must to the battle fly;

17. **secure:** free from care. 18. **over-lusty:** over-merry. 19. **low-rated:** undervalued. 25. **gesture sad:** sober bearing. 26. **Investing:** clothing. The figure is a favorite one with Shakespeare. Here the sober bearing of the men is spoken of as clothing their cheeks and coats, inasmuch as one's bearing is in a certain sense the garment which covers everything. 35. **note:** indication. 37. **dedicate one jot of colour,** etc.: he does not lose any of his freshness of complexion on account of the fact that he has been awake all night. 38. **all-watched night:** the night in which he has not slept at all. 39. **freshly looks:** looks fresh. The adverb was regular in Elizabethan English.—**overbears attaint:** conquers the natural exhausted appearance which one has who has not slept. 41. **That:** so that. 45. **mean and gentle all.** This may be either the vocative, addressed to the audience in the theater, or the nominative (the subject of *behold*), referring to the soldiers in the English army. The vocative construction is more probable, since the Chorus is giving an account of the scenes that are to come. *Mean* was not an offensive word. It simply meant 'persons of low degree.' 46. **as may unworthiness define:** so far as our poor and unworthy abilities can depict it.

Where, O for pity, we shall much disgrace
With four or five most vile and ragged foils,   50
Right ill-dispos'd in brawl ridiculous,
The name of Agincourt. Yet sit and see,
Minding true things by what their mock'ries be.   *Exit.*

SCENE I. *France. The English camp at Agincourt.*

Enter the King, Bedford, *and* Gloucester.

KING   Gloucester, 'tis true that we are in great danger;
The greater therefore should our courage be.
Good morrow, brother Bedford. God Almighty!
There is some soul of goodness in things evil,
Would men observingly distil it out.   5
For our bad neighbour makes us early stirrers,
Which is both healthful, and good husbandry.
Besides, they are our outward consciences,
And preachers to us all, admonishing
That we should dress us fairly for our end.   10
Thus may we gather honey from the weed
And make a moral of the devil himself.

Enter Erpingham.

Good morrow, old Sir Thomas Erpingham.
A good soft pillow for that good white head
Were better than a churlish turf of France.   15

ERP.   Not so, my liege. This lodging likes me better,
Since I may say 'Now lie I like a king.'

---

50. **foils:** persons armed with foils. Properly *foils* were blunted swords used in fencing; here the term is used contemptuously for the swords which the players carry. 51. **Right ill-disposed:** very ill-arranged. 52. **Yet:** despite the poorness of our representation. 53. **Minding true things,** etc.: seeing in our mind's eye the actual facts on the basis of the imitations which we present.

SCENE I.
In the scene that follows—'the little touch of Harry in the night'—the King has an interview with almost every kind of person in the host. First with a great noble, Gloucester; next with Sir Thomas Erpingham, a sturdy and honourable old knight; then with the rascally and boasting Pistol; again with Fluellen and Gower, two captains equally devoted to him, but of a different country; last of all, with the sturdy English private soldiers, Bates and Williams. It is worth noting, however, that, contradicting the Chorus, Henry only appears as himself, cheerful and supportive, to the "gentles." To the "mean" soldiers, he is either in disguise (Pistol, Bates and Williams) or out of sight (Gower and Fluellen). [A.C.] 4. **some soul of goodness:** some kernel or nucleus of goodness. 8. **our outward consciences:** they serve us in place of conscience, though they are external to us and not within, as consciences are. 10. **dress us fairly:** make ourselves well prepared. 14 ff. **good soft pillow,** etc. This remark, with Erpingham's answer, is historical. 15. **a churlish turf:** *churlish* means 'niggardly.' The French turf begrudges Erpingham a good night's sleep. 16. **likes me:** pleases me.

KING   'Tis good for men to love their present pains
                Upon example: so the spirit is eas'd;
                And when the mind is quick'ned, out of doubt   20
                The organs, though defunct and dead before,
                Break up their drowsy grave and newly move
                With casted slough and fresh legerity.
                Lend me thy cloak, Sir Thomas. Brothers both,
                Commend me to the princes in our camp;   25
                Do my good morrow to them, and anon
                Desire them all to my pavilion.

GLOUC.   We shall, my liege.

ERP.   Shall I attend your Grace?

KING   No, my good knight.
                Go with my brothers to my lords of England.   30
                I and my bosom must debate awhile,
                And then I would no other company.

ERP.   The Lord in heaven bless thee, noble Harry.

Exeunt [all but the King].

KING   God-a-mercy, old heart! thou speak'st cheerfully.

Enter Pistol.

PIST.   *Qui va là?*   35

KING   A friend.

PIST.   Discuss unto me, art thou officer;
                Or art thou base, common, and popular?

KING   I am a gentleman of a company.

PIST.   Trail'st thou the puissant pike?   40

KING   Even so. What are you?

PIST.   As good a gentleman as the Emperor.

KING   Then you are a better than the King.

PIST.   The King's a bawcock, and a heart of gold,

---

19. **Upon example:** for example, on account of example—i.e., by remembering some other person who endures the like. 21. **defunct and dead:** these two words mean practically the same thing—'paralyzed,' as it were. 23. **casted slough.** The figure is from a snake which casts its skin.—**legerity:** nimbleness, vigour. 25. **Commend me:** give my regards. 26. **Do my good morrow to them:** bid them good morrow in my name. 34. **God-a-mercy:** gramercy, many thanks. *Gramercy* is a corruption of *graunt mercy,* i.e., 'great thanks.' *God-a-mercy,* which properly means 'God have mercy,' has been confused with this phrase. 37. **Discuss unto me:** tell me. 38. **popular:** one of the common people. 39. **a gentleman of a company:** an inferior officer, a non-commissioned officer. 44. **bawcock:** fine fellow. A term used exclusively of men. Literally, fine cock.

	A lad of life, an imp of fame,	45
	Of parents good, of fist most valiant.	
	I kiss his dirty shoe, and from heartstring	
	I love the lovely bully. What is thy name?	

KING   Harry le Roy.

PIST.   Le Roy? A Cornish name. Art thou of Cornish crew?   50

KING   No, I am a Welshman.

PIST.   Know'st thou Fluellen?

KING   Yes.

PIST.   Tell him I'll knock his leek about his pate
        Upon Saint Davy's day.   55

KING   Do not you wear your dagger in your cap that day, lest he knock that
        about yours.

PIST.   Art thou his friend?

KING   And his kinsman too.

PIST.   The *figo* for thee then.   60

KING   I thank you. God be with you!

PIST.   My name is Pistol call'd.   *Exit, all except King.*

KING   It sorts well with your fierceness.

                    Enter Fluellen *and* Gower.

GOW.   Captain Fluellen!   64

FLU.   So! in the name of Jesu Christ, speak lower. It is the greatest admiration in
        the universal world, when the true and aunchient prerogatifes and laws of
        the wars is not kept. If you would take the pains but to examine the wars
        of Pompey the Great, you shall find, I warrant you, that there is no tiddle
        taddle nor pibble pabble in Pompey's camp. I warrant you, you shall find
        the ceremonies of the wars, and the cares of it, and the forms of it, and
        the sobriety of it, and the modesty of it, to be otherwise.   71

GOW.   Why, the enemy is loud; you hear him all night.

---

45. **A lad of life:** a lively lad.—**an imp of fame:** *imp* means 'scion,' and is often used for a young person. Hence *imp of fame* means 'a scion of a famous stock.' 48. **bully:** a slang term of endearment. 51. **a Welshman.** The King was born at Monmouth, in Wales. 59. **his kinsman.** The Welsh were famous for keeping their genealogical connections up to the remotest degree. Hence it is proverbial that all Welsh gentlemen are related. 63. **sorts well with:** well befits. 65. **So!** yes, I am he.—**speak lower.** Gower has hailed Fluellen in a loud voice on meeting him suddenly in the dark.—**admiration:** wonder. 66. **prerogatifes:** used here in the same sense as 'laws' or 'rules.' 69. **Pompey's camp.** Fluellen's example is unfortunate, inasmuch as Pompey's most famous camp, that just before the Battle of Pharsalia, was noted for its luxury and lack of discipline. No doubt Shakespeare knew this from his Plutarch, and intentionally makes Fluellen's learning go astray. 71. **modesty:** moderation—the same as 'sobriety.'

FLU.   If the enemy is an ass and a fool and a prating coxcomb, is it meet, think
         you, that we should also, look you, be an ass and a fool and a prating
         coxcomb? In your own conscience now?   75

GOW.   I will speak lower.

FLU.   I pray you and beseech you that you will.

                                              Exeunt [Gower and Fluellen].

KING   Though it appear a little out of fashion,
         There is much care and valor in this Welshman.

Enter three Soldiers, John Bates, Alexander Court, *and* Michael Williams.

COURT   Brother John Bates, is not that the morning which breaks yonder?   80

BATES   I think it be; but we have no great cause to desire the approach
         of day.

WILL.   We see yonder the beginning of the day, but I think we shall never see the
         end of it. Who goes there?

KING   A friend.   85

WILL.   Under what captain serve you?

KING   Under Sir Thomas Erpingham.

WILL.   A good old commander and a most kind gentleman. I pray you, what
         thinks he of our estate?

KING   Even as men wrack'd upon a sand, that look to be wash'd off the next
         tide.   91

BATES   He hath not told his thought to the King?

KING   No; nor is it not meet he should. For though I speak it to you, I think
         the King is but a man, as I am. The violet smells to him as it doth to me;
         the element shows to him as it doth to me; all his senses have but human
         conditions. His ceremonies laid by, in his nakedness he appears but a
         man; and though his affections are higher mounted than ours, yet, when
         they stoop, they stoop with the like wing. Therefore, when he sees reason
         of fears, as we do, his fears, out of doubt, be of the same relish as ours are.
         Yet, in reason, no man should possess him with any appearance of fear,
         lest he, by showing it, should dishearten his army.   101

---

78. **a little out of fashion:** a little quaint. 81. **I think it be.** This use of the subjunctive in indirect discourse
is not meant to imply any particular doubt. 89. **estate:** state, condition. 90. **a sand:** a sand bar. 95. **the
element:** the sky.—**shows:** appears, looks. 96. **conditions:** characters, qualities.—**ceremonies:** his clothes
of state, his splendid apparel. 97. **affections:** feelings.— **are higher mounted:** soar higher. 98. **stoop:**
descend in their flight.—**with the like wing:** in the same way, in similar flight. The language of this
metaphor is taken from the technical vocabulary of falconry. 99. **out of doubt:** beyond question.—**be of
the same relish:** taste the same way to him—i.e., when the King feels, his feeling is like ours, though when
he hopes, his hopes may be higher than ours. 100. **no man should possess him with any appearance of
fear:** no man should put the King in possession of (i.e., let the King see) any appearance of fear in him.

BATES   He may show what outward courage he will; but I believe, as cold a night
         as 'tis, he could wish himself in Thames up to the neck; and so I would he
         were, and I by him, at all adventures, so we were quit here.

KING   By my troth, I will speak my conscience of the King: I think he would not
         wish himself anywhere but where he is.   106

BATES   Then I would he were here alone. So should he be sure to be ransomed,
         and a many poor men's lives saved.

KING   I dare say you love him not so ill to wish him here alone, howsoever you
         speak this to feel other men's minds. Methinks I could not die anywhere
         so contented as in the King's company, his cause being just and his quarrel
         honorable.

WILL.   That's more than we know.

BATES   Ay, or more than we should seek after; for we know enough if we know
         we are the King's subjects. If his cause be wrong, our obedience to the
         King wipes the crime of it out of us.   116

WILL.   But if the cause be not good, the King himself hath a heavy reckoning
         to make when all those legs and arms and heads, chopp'd off in a battle,
         shall join together at the latter day and cry all 'We died at such a place!'
         some swearing, some crying for a surgeon, some upon their wives left
         poor behind them, some upon the debts they owe, some upon their
         children rawly left. I am afeard there are few die well that die in a battle;
         for how can they charitably dispose of anything when blood is their
         argument? Now, if these men do not die well, it will be a black matter for
         the King that led them to it; who to disobey were against all proportion
         of subjection.   126

KING   So, if a son that is by his father sent about merchandise do sinfully miscarry
         upon the sea, the imputation of his wickedness, by your rule, should be

---

104. **at all adventures:** at all hazards. Bates means that he would take the risk of being in the Thames up to
the neck rather than the risk of being in his present situation. 105. **my conscience:** what I really think.
109. **to wish:** as to wish. 111. **his cause being just,** etc. The King 's confidence in the justice of his
cause is insisted on with good effect here. Our minds revert to the elaborate discussion of this question
at the beginning of the play.—**quarrel:** the cause for which one contends. 119. **the latter day:** the day
of judgment. 120. **some swearing,** etc.: i.e., the owners of the legs and arms referred to.—**some upon
their wives:** i.e., some crying out upon their wives. *To cry out upon* sometimes means 'to cry out against'
and sometimes, as here, merely 'to mention by way of lamentation or regret.' 122. **rawly left:** left in poor
circumstances. *Raw* means 'not provided for.' We have the same use of the word in *Macbeth*, iv, 1, 26: 'Why
in that rawness left you wife and child,' i.e., why did you leave your wife and children in so unprepared and
defenseless a state? Note that the adverb *rawly* is precisely equivalent to 'in rawness.' The use of an adverb
in *-ly* to express condition rather than manner is common.—**afeared.** Now rustic, but not so then.—**die
well:** i.e., make a good end, die a Christian death. 123. **charitably dispose of anything:** make such a
disposition of their affairs as accords with Christian charity—i.e., forgive enemies, etc. 124. **argument:**
the whole subject of their thoughts at the time. 125. **all proportion of subjection:** all propriety or reason
on the part of his subjects. 127. **sent about merchandise:** sent on a trading voyage. [A.C.]—**do sinfully
miscarry upon the sea:** is lost at sea while in a state of sin.

imposed upon his father that sent him; or if a servant, under his master's command transporting a sum of money, be assailed by robbers and die in many irreconcil'd iniquities, you may call the business of the master the author of the servant's damnation. But this is not so. The King is not bound to answer the particular endings of his soldiers, the father of his son, nor the master of his servant; for they purpose not their death when they purpose their services. Besides, there is no king, be his cause never so spotless, if it come to the arbitrement of swords, can try it out with all unspotted soldiers. Some (peradventure) have on them the guilt of premeditated and contrived murther; some, of beguiling virgins with the broken seals of perjury; some, making the wars their bulwark, that have before gored the gentle bosom of peace with pillage and robbery. Now, if these men have defeated the law and outrun native punishment, though they can outstrip men, they have no wings to fly from God. War is his beadle, war is his vengeance; so that here men are punish'd for before-breach of the King's laws in now the King's quarrel. Where they feared the death, they have borne life away; and where they would be safe, they perish. Then if they die unprovided, no more is the King guilty of their damnation than he was before guilty of those impieties for the which they are now visited. Every subject's duty is the King's, but every subject's soul is his own. Therefore should every soldier in the wars do as every sick man in his bed—wash every mote out of his conscience; and dying so, death is to him advantage; or not dying, the time was blessedly lost wherein such preparation was gained; and in him that escapes, it were not sin to think that, making God so free an offer, he let him outlive that day to see his greatness and to teach others how they should prepare.   154

WILL.   'Tis certain, every man that dies ill, the ill upon his own head—the King is not to answer it.

BATES   I do not desire he should answer for me, and yet I determine to fight lustily for him.

KING   I myself heard the King say he would not be ransom'd.   159

---

131. **in many irreconciled iniquities:** with many sins upon his conscience for which he has not made his peace with God. 133. **to answer the particular endings of his soldiers:** to be responsible for the particular way in which each of his soldiers meets his death—i.e., whether in a condition of harmony with God or the reverse. 134. **they:** i.e., the King , the father, the master. 136. **arbitrement:** judgment, decision. 137. **all unspotted soldiers:** with soldiers, none of whom shall be stained with guilt. 139. **the broken seals of perjury:** perjury itself is the act of breaking the seal of an oath.—**making the wars their bulwark:** hiding behind the defense of warfare. Taking advantage, in other words, of a warlike time, these soldiers have inflicted injury on non-combatants or peaceable citizens. 141. **outrun native punishment:** escaped punishment in their native land. 143. **beadle:** an officer whose duty it is to arrest and punish for various offenses. 146. **unprovided:** unprepared for death. 148. **visited:** visited with God's vengeance, punished.—**Every subject's duty is the King 's:** the King has a right to the duty of every subject. 150. **mote:** least spot—a manifest allusion to the parable of the mote and the beam.—**dying so:** i.e., dying with a clean conscience. 153. **making God so free an offer:** since he offered his soul so freely to the Lord. 155. **'Tis certain,** etc. Williams is convinced by the King 's logic and sums up the argument in complete assent with him. 158. **lustily:** vigorously.

WILL.   Ay, he said so, to make us fight cheerfully; but when our throats are cut, he may be ransom'd, and we ne'er the wiser.

KING   If I live to see it, I will never trust his word after.

WILL.   You pay him then! That's a perilous shot out of an elder-gun that a poor and a private displeasure can do against a monarch. You may as well go about to turn the sun to ice with fanning in his face with a peacock's feather. You'll never trust his word after! Come, 'tis a foolish saying. 166

KING   Your reproof is something too round. I should be angry with you if the time were convenient.†

WILL.   Let it be a quarrel between us, if you live.

KING   I embrace it.   170

WILL.   How shall I know thee again?

KING   Give me any gage of thine, and I will wear it in my bonnet. Then, if ever thou dar'st acknowledge it, I will make it my quarrel.

WILL.   Here's my glove. Give me another of thine.

KING   There.   175

WILL.   This will I also wear in my cap. If ever thou come to me and say, after tomorrow, 'This is my glove,' by this hand, I will take thee a box on the ear.

KING   If ever I live to see it, I will challenge it.

WILL.   Thou dar'st as well be hang'd.   180

KING   Well, I will do it, though I take thee in the King's company.

WILL.   Keep thy word. Fare thee well.

BATES   Be friends, you English fools, be friends! We have French quarrels enow, if you could tell how to reckon.

KING   Indeed the French may lay twenty French crowns to one they will beat us, for they bear them on their shoulders; but it is no English treason to cut French crowns, and tomorrow the King himself will be a clipper.   187

---

163. **You pay him then!** Said very sarcastically—'That will be a terrible punishment for him, won't it!'— **an elder-gun:** a pop-gun made out of an elder stick with the pith taken out. 165. **go about:** undertake. 167. **round:** outspoken, blunt. 168. **convenient:** fitting. 172. **gage:** pledge.—**bonnet:** cap. 177. **take:** give. 183. **enow:** enough. Often used as a plural, but not exclusively so. 185. **lay:** bet. The pun on *crowns* is obvious. 186, 187. **to cut French crowns:** the two senses are (1) to clip the coins known as French crowns; (2) to cut French heads with the sword.—**a clipper.** This carries out the pun. A person who cut off small pieces of coin so as to make them under weight was called a clipper. The punishment for this was death. It was easy to clip coins in old times, because they were not exactly round and had not milled edges as at the present day.

---

† Productions vary on how heated this argument becomes, and whether Henry is the instigator or not. Each option presents a different view of Henry on the eve of battle. [A.C.]

Exeunt Soldiers.

Upon the King. Let us our lives, our souls,
Our debts, our careful wives,
Our children, and our sins, lay on the King.   190
We must bear all. O hard condition,
Twin-born with greatness, subject to the breath
Of every fool, whose sense no more can feel
But his own wrlnging. What infinite heart's ease
Must kings neglect that private men enjoy!   195
And what have kings that privates have not too,
Save ceremony, save general ceremony?
And what art thou, thou idol Ceremony?
What kind of god art thou, that suffer'st more
Of mortal griefs than do thy worshippers?   200
What are thy rents? What are thy comings-in?
O Ceremony, show me but thy worth.
What is thy soul of adoration?
Art thou aught else but place, degree, and form,
Creating awe and fear in other men?   205
Wherein thou art less happy being fear'd
Than they in fearing.
What drink'st thou oft, instead of homage sweet,
But poison'd flattery? O, be sick, great greatness,
And bid thy ceremony give thee cure.   210
Think'st thou the fiery fever will go out
With titles blown from adulation?
Will it give place to flexure and low bending?
Canst thou, when thou command'st the beggar's knee,
Command the health of it? No, thou proud dream,   215
That play'st so subtly with a king's repose.
I am a king that find thee, and I know.
'Tis not the balm, the sceptre, and the ball,

---

189. **careful:** anxious. 192. **subject.** This agrees with *greatness*. Majesty itself is subject to the foolish talk of everybody. 193. **sense:** sensibility, sensitiveness. 194. **his own wringing:** that which pinches him. *To wring* was 'to pinch' or 'to twist.' There is doubtless an allusion to the old proverb 'I know best myself where my shoe wrings me,' or, as we say now, 'where the shoe pinches.'—**heart's-ease:** a beautiful old word for 'contentment.' 195. **neglect:** disregard, pass by, do without—not implying any culpability, as is the case today with the word. 197. **ceremony:** used in the most general sense for 'pomp and all that attends rank.' 201. **comings-in:** income. 203. **thy soul of adoration:** that essential quality which makes thee so much adored. 209. **great greatness.** The repetition, like plays on words in general, here expresses contempt. 212. **blown.** Words are but breath, and breath is but air; hence it is common to find all sorts of words appropriate to wind used of speech. 213. **give place to:** give way to, retire before.—**flexure:** means the same thing as 'low bending.' 215. **thou proud dream.** The King is still addressing ceremony. 216. **play'st so subtly with a King's repose:** cheats a King so cleverly out of his repose. 217. **find thee:** find thee out, detect thy real nature. 218. **balm:** i.e., the holy oil with which Kings are anointed at their coronation.—**the ball:** i.e., the apple or globe, a figure of universal sovereignty.

The sword, the mace, the crown imperial,
The intertissued robe of gold and pearl,   220
The farced title running fore the king,
The throne he sits on, nor the tide of pomp
That beats upon the high shore of this world—
No, not all these, thrice-gorgeous ceremony,
Not all these, laid in bed majestical,   225
Can sleep so soundly as the wretched slave,
Who, with a body fill'd, and vacant mind,
Gets him to rest, cramm'd with distressful bread;
Never sees horrid night, the child of hell;
But like a lackey, from the rise to set,   230
Sweats in the eye of Phœbus, and all night
Sleeps in Elysium; next day after dawn,
Doth rise and help Hyperion to his horse;
And follows so the ever-running year
With profitable labor to his grave;   235
And but for ceremony, such a wretch,
Winding up days with toil and nights with sleep,
Had the forehand and vantage of a king.
The slave, a member of the country's peace,
Enjoys it, but in gross brain little wots   240
What watch the king keeps to maintain the peace,
Whose hours the peasant best advantages.

Enter Erpingham.

ERP.   My lord, your nobles, jealous of your absence,
         Seek through your camp to find you.

---

220. **The intertissued robe of gold and pearl:** the coronation mantle interwoven with gold and pearls. 221. **The farced title:** the stuffed title; hence, the long and elaborate title. The word *farced* expresses contempt. The title is said to run before the King by a lively figure. Just as the person who announces the coming of the King runs before him to clear the way, so the title may be said to precede the King wherever he goes. 222. **the tide of pomp:** i.e., the flood tide of splendid ceremony. 224, 225. Note the variation of accent in the phrase *all these*. This accords with a common trick of Elizabethan metre. 225 ff. Note the similarity of Henry V's reflection on sleep to that of his father in *2 Henry IV*, iii, 1. 227. **vacant:** free from care. 228. **distressful bread:** bread gained by hard labour. 233. **Hyperion:** the sun. In order to help Hyperion harness his horses one must, of course, rise before dawn. 237. **Winding up:** occupying and closing. 238. **forehand:** advantage. *Vantage* in the same line is a synonym. 239. **a member of the country's peace:** i.e., a person who belongs to a peaceable and well-ordered community. 240. **it:** i.e., the peace which the King maintains.—**gross:** stupid.—**wots:** knows. 242. **Whose hours the peasant best advantages.** *Advantages*, though in the singular, seems to have *hours* for its subject and *peasant* for its object. The usual meaning of *vantage*, when a verb, is 'to profit,' 'to be for the advantage of.' It is conceivable, however, that *peasant* is the subject and *hours* the object, in which case *hours* must be taken as meaning 'gets the profit of,' 'profits by.' To have a plural noun and a singular verb was very common in Elizabethan English. 243. **jealous of your absence:** suspecting, because of your absence, that some harm has come to you. *Jealous* regularly equals 'suspicious.'

KING   Good old knight,
    Collect them all together at my tent.   245
    I'll be before thee.

ERP.   I shall do't, my lord.   *Exit.*

KING   O God of battles, steel my soldiers' hearts,
    Possess them not with fear! Take from them now
    The sense of reck'ning, if th' opposed numbers
    Pluck their hearts from them. Not today, O Lord,   250
    O, not today, think not upon the fault
    My father made in compassing the crown!
    I Richard's body have interred new;
    And on it have bestowed more contrite tears
    Than from it issued forced drops of blood.   255
    Five hundred poor I have in yearly pay,
    Who twice a day their wither'd hands hold up
    Toward heaven, to pardon blood; and I have built
    Two chantries, where the sad and solemn priests
    Sing still for Richard's soul. More will I do.   260
    Though all that I can do is nothing worth,
    Since that my penitence comes after all,
    Imploring pardon.

Enter Gloucester.

GLOUC.   My liege.

KING   · My brother Gloucester's voice? Ay.   265
    I know thy errand; I will go with thee.
    The day, my friends, and all things stay for me.   *Exeunt.*

SCENE II. *The French camp.*

Enter the Dauphin, Orleans, Rambures, *and* Beaumont.

ORL.   The sun doth gild our armor. Up, my lords!

---

246. **I shall do't.** The most courteous form of assent in Elizabethan English was *I shall* rather than *I will*, because *I shall* suggests that obedience is *inevitable*, a matter of course, and not dependent on the speaker's volition. 247. What follows shows the King in a devout mood. 249. **The sense of reckoning:** the ability to count or reckon. 251, 252. **the fault My father made.** *To make a fault* was a regular Elizabethan idiom, from the French *faire une faute.* The usurpation of the throne and the subsequent murder of Richard II by Henry IV is meant. [A.C.]—**compassing:** getting possession of. 259. **chantries:** chapels for the performance of special masses for the souls of the dead. They were usually attached to a cathedral church. 260. **still:** ever, without ceasing.

SCENE II.
This scene is merely the conclusion of the last scene in Act III. The day, so longed for by the French nobles, has dawned at last. 1. **Up:** not 'rise from sleep,' of course, but 'to horse.' 2. **Montez a cheval!:** To horse! [A.C.]

Dau.	*Montez à cheval!* My horse! *Varlet, laquais!* Ha!
Orl.	O brave spirit!
Dau.	*Via! les eaux et la terre—*
Orl.	*Rien puis? L'air et le feu.* 5
Dau.	*Ciel!* cousin Orleans.

Enter Constable.

	Now, my Lord Constable?
Con.	Hark how our steeds for present service neigh!
Dau.	Mount them and make incision in their hides,
	That their hot blood may spin in English eyes 10
	And dout them with superfluous courage, ha!
Ram.	What, will you have them weep our horses' blood?
	How shall we then behold their natural tears?

Enter Messenger.

Mess.	The English are embattail'd, you French peers.
Con.	To horse, you gallant princes! straight to horse! 15
	Do but behold yond poor and starved band,
	And your fair show shall suck away their souls,
	Leaving them but the shales and husks of men.
	There is not work enough for all our hands,
	Scarce blood enough in all their sickly veins 20
	To give each naked curtleaxe a stain
	That our French gallants shall to-day draw out
	And sheathe for lack of sport. Let us but blow on them,
	The vapor of our valour will o'erturn them.
	'Tis positive 'gainst all exceptions, lords, 25
	That our superfluous lackeys and our peasants,
	Who in unnecessary action swarm
	About our squares of battle, were enow
	To purge this field of such a hilding foe,

Varlet: valet. The same as *laquais*, 'lackey.' 4. **Via!** on! 4, 5. **les eaux et la terre–Rien puis? L'air et le feu.**: This dialogue is not entirely clear, but probably refers back to the Dauphin's claim that his horse has only two of the four elements, and indicates something like 'Away waters and earth' (from ourselves). 'Nothing afterwards [but] fire and air?' 'Nothing.' [A.C.] 10. **in:** into. 11. **dout them:** put them (the eyes) out (from *do out*; like *don* from *do on*, *doff* from *do off*, *dup* from *do up*).—**with superfluous courage:** with the blood which they have in greater abundance than is necessary. Courage and fullness of blood were thought to go together. The horses, having a superabundance of courage, may well spare some of their blood. 14. **embattailed:** drawn up in battle array. 17. **fair show:** gallant appearance. 21. **curtleaxe:** cutlass. 25. **'Tis positive 'gainst all exceptions:** it may be asserted positively in defiance of all objection or contradiction. Cf. the phrase *to take exception* for 'to object.' 29. **hilding:** wretched, insignificant. Used either as a noun or as an adjective.

Though we upon this mountain's basis by   30
Took stand for idle speculation:
But that our honours must not. What's to say?
A very little little let us do,
And all is done. Then let the trumpets sound
The tucket sonance and the note to mount,   35
For our approach shall so much dare the field
That England shall couch down in fear and yield.

Enter Grandpré.

GRAND.   Why do you stay so long, my lords of France?
Yond island carrions, desperate of their bones,
Ill-favouredly become the morning field.   40
Their ragged curtains poorly are let loose,
And our air shakes them passing scornfully.
Big Mars seems bankrout in their beggar'd host
And faintly through a rusty beaver peeps.
The horsemen sit like fixed candlesticks   45
With torch-staves in their hand; and their poor jades
Lob down their heads, dropping the hides and hips,
The gum down roping from their pale-dead eyes,
And in their pale dull mouths the gimmal'd bit
Lies foul with chaw'd grass, still and motionless.   50
And their executors, the knavish crows,
Fly o'er them, all impatient for their hour.
Description cannot suit itself in words
To demonstrate the life of such a battle
In life so liveless as it shows itself.   55

CON.   They have said their prayers, and they stay for death.

DAU.   Shall we go send them dinners and fresh suits
And give their fasting horses provender,
And after fight with them?

CON.   I stay but for my guidon. To the field!   60

---

31. **speculation:** looking on. 35. **tucket sonance:** the signal to mount [A.C.] 36. **dare:** frighten. 37. **couch:** crouch. 39. **desperate of their bones:** without hope of saving themselves, poor skeletons that they are. 40. **Ill-favouredly,** etc.: i.e., these scarecrows are a disfigurement to the fair landscape and ought to be cleared away. 42. **passing:** surpassingly, very. 43. **Big:** threatening. The idea is that they look like a troop of military bankrupts—so poverty-stricken is their appearance. 44. **beaver:** the moveable part of the helmet. 45. **candlesticks:** ornamental candlesticks, etc., often had the form of horsemen, lance in hand. 47. **Lob:** lop, hang dejectedly. 49. **gimmaled:** jointed. 50. **motionless.** They have not life enough to chew grass. 51. **executors:** possibly, executioners (as in i, 2, 203); but more probably in the modern sense—as executors settle the estates of dead men, so the crows will pick the bones of these horses (or horses and soldiers)—all they have to leave behind them. 53. **suit itself in words:** clothe itself in fitting terms. 54. **To demonstrate the life of such a battle:** to describe such an army *to the life*. Note the scornful playing on the word *life* in the next verse. 60. **guidon:** the pennant or little banner fixed to a staff—his official sign as commander.

I will the banner from a trumpet take
And use it for my haste. Come, come away.
The sun is high, and we outwear the day.   *Exeunt.*

SCENE III. *The English camp.*

Enter Gloucester, Bedford, Exeter, Erpingham *with all his host,*
Salisbury, *and* Westmoreland.

GLOUC.   Where is the King?

BED.   The King himself is rode to view their battle.

WEST.   Of fighting men they have full threescore thousand.

EXE.   There's five to one; besides, they all are fresh.

SAL.   God's arm strike with us! 'Tis a fearful odds.   5
God b' wi' you, princes all; I'll to my charge.
If we no more meet till we meet in heaven,
Then joyfully, my noble Lord of Bedford,
My dear Lord Gloucester, and my good Lord Exeter,
And my kind kinsman, warriors all, *adieu!*   10

BED.   Farewell, good Salisbury, and good luck go with thee.

EXE.   Farewell, kind lord. Fight valiantly today;
And yet I do thee wrong to mind thee of it,
For thou art fram'd of the firm truth of valor.   [*Exit Salisbury.*]

BED.   He is as full of valor as of kindness,   15
Princely in both.

Enter the King.

WEST.   O that we now had here
But one ten thousand of those men in England
That do no work today!

KING   What's he that wishes so?
My cousin Westmoreland? No, my fair cousin.
If we arc mark'd to die, we are enough   20
To do our country loss; and if to live,
The fewer men, the greater share of honor.
God's will! I pray thee wish not one man more.

---

61. **banner:** the streamer affixed to a trumpet.—**trumpet:** trumpeter. 63. **outwear:** waste in idleness.
SCENE III.
2. **battle:** army drawn up. 6. **charge:** troop, division. 23. **God's will!** Comparing this interjection with *By Jove* in the next verse, Dr. Johnson remarks that 'the King prays like a Christian and swears like a heathen.'

By Jove, I am not covetous for gold,
Nor care I who doth feed upon my cost;   25
It yearns me not if men my garments wear;
Such outward things dwell not in my desires:
But if it be a sin to covet honor,
I am the most offending soul alive.
No, faith, my coz, wish not a man from England.   30
God's peace. I would not lose so great an honor
As one man more methinks would share from me
For the best hope I have. O, do not wish one more!
Rather proclaim it, Westmoreland, through my host,
That he which hath no stomach to this fight,   35
Let him depart; his passport shall be made,
And crowns for convoy put into his purse.
We would not die in that man's company
That fears his fellowship to die with us.
This day is call'd the Feast of Crispian.   40
He that outlives this day, and comes safe home,
Will stand a-tiptoe when this day is nam'd
And rouse him at the name of Crispian.
He that shall live this day, and see old age,
Will yearly on the vigil feast his neighbours   45
And say 'Tomorrow is Saint Crispian.'
Then will he strip his sleeve and show his scars,
And say 'These wounds I had on Crispin's day.'
Old men forget; yet all shall be forgot,
But he'll remember, with advantages,   50
What feats he did that day. Then shall our names,
Familiar in his mouth as household words—
Harry the King, Bedford and Exeter,
Warwick and Talbot, Salisbury and Gloucester—
Be in their flowing cups freshly rememb'red.   55
This story shall the good man teach his son;
And Crispin Crispian shall ne'er go by,
From this day to the ending of the world,
But we in it shall be remembered.
We few, we happy few, we band of brothers;   60
For he today that sheds his blood with me

---

26. **It yearns me not:** it does not trouble me. 36. **passport:** discharge and free conduct. 37. **convoy:** traveling expenses. 39. **fears his fellowship to die with us:** is afraid to grant me his company by dying with me. 42. **a-tiptoe:** on tiptoe (with enthusiasm). 44. **live:** outlive. 45. **the vigil:** the vigil of a feast is the eve of the feast day, the night before it, which was celebrated with merriment. 50. **with advantages:** with additions, with exaggeration. 57. **Crispin Crispian.** The Battle of Agincourt was fought on the day of St. Crispin and St. Crispian.

Shall be my brother. Be he ne'er so vile,
This day shall gentle his condition;
And gentlemen in England now abed
Shall think themselves accurs'd they were not here, 65
And hold their manhoods cheap whiles any speaks
That fought with us upon Saint Crispin's day.

Enter Salisbury.

SAL.   My sovereign lord, bestow yourself with speed.
The French are bravely in their battles set
And will with all expedience charge on us.   70

KING   All things are ready, if our minds be so.

WEST.   Perish the man whose mind is backward now!

KING   Thou dost not wish more help from England, coz?

WEST.   God's will, my liege! would you and I alone,
Without more help, could fight this royal battle.   75

KING   Why, now thou hast unwish'd five thousand men.
Which likes me better than to wish us one.
You know your places. God be with you all!

Tucket. Enter Montjoy.

MONT.   Once more I come to know of thee, King Harry,
If for thy ransom thou wilt now compound,   80
Before thy most assured overthrow;
For certainly thou art so near the gulf
Thou needs must be englutted. Besides, in mercy,
The Constable desires thee thou wilt mind
Thy followers of repentance, that their souls   85
May make a peaceful and a sweet retire
From all these fields, where (wretches) their poor bodies
Must lie and fester.

KING   Who hath sent thee now?

MONT.   The Constable of France.

KING   I pray thee bear my former answer back: 90

---

62. **vile:** of low birth. 63. **gentle his condition:** give him the rank of a gentleman. 68. **bestow yourself:** take up your position. 69. **bravely:** finely, handsomely—referring to the splendid appearance that they make.—**battles:** battalions. 70. **expedience:** speed. 76. **unwished five thousand men.** The English had about ten thousand men. The King's arithmetic has given the commentators some trouble. Apparently he regards himself and Westminster as each representing half of the English forces (as would indeed be the case if the two fought the battle alone), and thinks of Westminster as having wished his own half out of existence. But the passage is far from clear. 77. **likes:** pleases. 80. **compound:** settle, make arrangements. 82. **gulf:** whirlpool. 83. **englutted:** swallowed up. 84. **mind:** remind. 88. **fester:** rot.

Fig. 2: Olivier's battle scene features a huge cast but very little fighting, no doubt because the film was made during the real fighting of World War II. © United Artists / Photofest.

Bid them achieve me, and then sell my bones.
Good God! why should they mock poor fellows thus?
The man that once did sell the lion's skin
While the beast liv'd, was kill'd with hunting him.
A many of our bodies shall no doubt   95
Find native graves; upon the which, I trust,
Shall witness live in brass of this day's work;
And those that leave their valiant bones in France,
Dying like men, though buried in your dunghills,
They shall be fam'd; for there the sun shall greet them   100
And draw their honors reeking up to heaven,
Leaving their earthly parts to choke your clime,
The smell whereof shall breed a plague in France.
Mark then abounding valour in our English,
That, being dead, like to the bullet's grazing,   105
Break out into a second course of mischief,
Killing in relapse of mortality.
Let me speak proudly. Tell the Constable
We are but warriors for the working day.
Our gayness and our gilt are all besmirch'd   110
With rainy marching in the painful field.
There's not a piece of feather in our host—
Good argument, I hope, we will not fly—
And time hath worn us into slovenry.
But, by the mass, our hearts are in the trim.   115
And my poor soldiers tell me, yet ere night

91. **achieve:** win, get possession of. 107. **in relapse of mortality:** by a kind of indirect deadliness.

Fig. 3: Branagh shows an exhausted and bloody Henry and Exeter after the battle, highlighting the physical and personal cost of war. © Renaissance Films/BBC/Curzon Films/ The Kobal Collection.

> They'll be in fresher robes, or they will pluck
> The gay new coats o'er the French soldiers' heads
> And turn them out of service. If they do this,
> As, if God please, they shall, my ransom then   120
> Will soon be levied. Herald, save thou thy labor.
> Come thou no more for ransom, gentle herald.
> They shall have none, I swear, but these my joints;
> Which if they have as I will leave 'em them,
> Shall yield them little; tell the Constable.   125

MONT.	I shall, King Harry. And so fare thee well.	
	Thou never shalt hear herald any more.	*Exit.*
KING	I fear thou wilt once more come again for ransom.	

Enter York.

YORK	My lord, most humbly on my knee I beg	
	The leading of the vaward.	130
KING	Take it, brave York. Now, soldiers, march away;	
	And how thou pleasest, God, dispose the day!†	*Exeunt.*

---

117. **They'll be,** etc.: they'll have fresher clothing (in some other way) or else they'll pull off the French coats for their own use—or, as we should say, they'll have fresher attire even if they have to pull off the French soldiers' coats to get it. 119. **turn them out of service.** With a pun, as if the French soldiers were servants in livery. 124. **as I will leave 'em them:** in the dilapidated condition in which they will be before I fall. 130. **vaward:** van.

---

† Shakespeare's play does not include any actual battle scenes to follow up on this stirring and heroic speech, but modern productions have been unable to resist adding them. The reason Shakespeare did not include battles is not because he couldn't stage them—he had duels and other forms of fighting in a number of plays, including *Henry IV:I*. [A.C.]

SCENE IV. *The field of battle.*†

Alarum. Excursions. Enter Pistol, French Soldier, Boy.

PIST.   Yield, cur!

FRENCH   *Je pense que vous estes le gentil-homme de bonne qualité.*

PIST.   Quality! *Callino custore me!* Art thou a gentleman? What is thy name?
         Discuss.

FRENCH   *O Seigneur Dieu!*   5

PIST.   O Signieur Dew should be a gentleman.
         Perpend my words, O Signieur Dew, and mark.
         O Signieur Dew, thou diest on point of fox,
         Except, O signieur, thou do give to me
         Egregious ransom.   10

FRENCH   *O, prenez miséricorde! ayez pitié de moi!*

PIST.   Moy shall not serve. I will have forty moys;
         Or I will fetch thy rim out at thy throat
         In drops of crimson blood.

FRENCH   *Est-il impossible d'eschapper la force de ton bras?*   15

PIST.   Brass, cur?
         Thou damned and luxurious mountain goat,
         Offer'st me brass?

SCENE IV.
In Henry's time, war was profitable business since soldiers of quality could expect to be held hostage for ransom rather than killed (cf Montjoy's repeated requests for Henry's ransom offer, and Williams' belief that Henry only pretends he will not be ransomed). This practice is here parodied savagely. [A.C.] 2. **Je pense** etc.: 'I think that you are a gentleman of good quality.' [A.C.] 3. **Callino custore me!** Pistol does not understand French, but he catches the word *qualité* and echoes it in a distorted form, adding some strange words of his own. Malone conjectured that *calmie custure me* is a misprint for *Calen, o custure me*, which Boswell corrected further to *Callino, castore me*. These words appear to be the refrain of an Irish song and perhaps we should restore them here. But it is perilous to emend Pistol's gibberish, and we have no warrant for supposing that he would not murder Irish as badly as he murders French in this play and Italian in *2 Henry IV*. He probably means to express contempt and to make an impression on the Frenchmen. 4. **Discuss:** declare. 6. **Signieur Dew.** Pistol takes the Frenchman's terrified exclamation (*Lord God!*) as a reply to his demand for his name. He recognizes *Seigneur* as meaning 'Lord,' and infers that his prisoner must be a gentleman. 7. **Perpend:** attend to, ponder. 8. **fox:** sword—so called because those made of a particularly good kind of steel had the figure of a fox as a trade-mark on the blade. 11. **O prenez** etc.: O take mercy. Have pity on me! [A.C.] 12. **Moy:** this Pistol takes as a sum of money or a coin. Some suppose he is thinking of a *moidore*, a Portuguese gold coin. 13. **rim:** midriff, diaphragm. 15. **Est-il** etc.: Is it impossible to escape the strength of your arm? [A.C.] 16. **Brass.** The *s* in *bras* was pronounced in early seventeenth-century French, so that Pistol's error is not unnatural—for him! 17. **luxurious:** lascivious.

---

†   Both Olivier and Branagh cut this scene, and although the BBC version retains it, several moments of fierce, extratextual fighting precede it. [A.C.]

FRENCH	*O, pardonnez-moi!*	
PIST.	Say'st thou me so? Is that a ton of moys?	20

PIST.   Say'st thou me so? Is that a ton of moys?   20
            Come hither, boy; ask me this slave in French
            What is his name.

BOY   *Escoutez. Comment estes-vous appelé?*

FRENCH   *Monsieur le Fer.*

BOY   He says his name is Master Fer.   25

PIST.   Master Fer? I'll fer him, and firk him, and ferret him! Discuss the same in
            French unto him.

BOY   I do not know the French for 'fer,' and 'ferret,' and 'firk.'

PIST.   Bid him prepare, for I will cut his throat.

FRENCH   *Que dit-il, monsieur?*   30

BOY   *Il me commande à vous dire que vous faites vous prest; care ce soldat ici est
            disposé tout à cette heure de couper vostre gorge.*

PIST.   Owy, cuppele gorge, permafoy!
            Peasant, unless thou give me crowns, brave crowns;
            Or mangled shalt thou be by this my sword.   35

FRENCH   *O, je vous supplie, pour l'amour de Dieu, me pardonner! Je suis gentilhomme
            de bonne maison. Gardez ma vie, et je vous donnerai deux cents escus.*

PIST.   What are his words?

BOY   He prays you to save his life. He is a gentleman of a good house, and for
            his ransom he will give you two hundred crowns.   40

PIST.   Tell him my fury shall abate, and I
            The crowns will take.

FRENCH   *Petit monsieur, que dit-il?*

BOY   *Encore qu'il est contre son jurement de pardonner aucun prisonnier,
            néantmoins, pour les escus que vous l'avez promis, il est content de vous
            donner la liberté, le franchisement.*   46

FRENCH.   *Sur mes genoux je vous donne mille remercîmens; et je m'estime heureux que
            je suis tombé entre les mains d'un chevalier, je pense, le plus brave, vaillant,
            et très-distingué seigneur d'Angleterre.*

PIST.   Expound unto me, boy.   50

---

19. **O, pardonnez-moi!**: More probably 'O spare me!' than the modern sense of 'excuse me.' The rest of
the French in this scene is translated by the Boy. [A.C.] 26. **I'll fer him.** Pistol simply repeats the soldier's
name with a threatening air. 33. **cuppele gorge.** This bit of broken French Pistol had learned before he
set out for the war. Cf. II.i.57: 'Couple a gorge! That is the word.' 34. **brave:** fine. 36. **O, je vous supplie,**
etc. The Frenchman does not understand Pistol's lingo,—except 'Owy, cuppele gorge,'—but he finds his
ferocious gestures intelligible enough.

BOY   He gives you, upon his knees, a thousand thanks; and he esteems himself happy that he hath fall'n into the hands of one (as he thinks) the most brave, valorous, and thrice-worthy signieur of England.

PIST.   As I suck blood, I will some mercy show!
Follow me, cur.   [*Exit.*]   55

BOY   *Suivez-vous le grand Capitaine.* [*Exit French Soldier.*] I did never know so full a voice issue from so empty a heart, but the saying is true, 'The empty vessel makes the greatest sound.' Bardolph and Nym had ten times more valour than this roaring devil i' th' old play that every one may pare his nails with a wooden dagger; and they are both hang'd; and so would this be, if he durst steal anything adventurously. I must stay with the lackeys with the luggage of our camp. The French might have a good prey of us, if he knew of it; for there is none to guard it but boys.   *Exit.*   63

SCENE V. *Another part of the field of battle.*

Enter Constable, Orleans, Bourbon, Dauphin, *and* Rambures.

CON.   *O diable!*

ORL.   *O Seigneur! le jour est perdu, tout est perdu!*

DAU.   *Mort de ma vie!* all is confounded, all!
Reproach and everlasting shame
Sits mocking in our plumes.

A short alarum.

O méchante fortune! Do not run away.   5

CON.   Why, all our ranks are broke.

DAU.   O perdurable shame! Let's stab ourselves.
Be these the wretches that we play'd at dice for?

ORL.   Is this the king we sent to for his ransom?

BOUR.   Shame, and eternal shame! nothing but shame!   10
Let's die in honor. Once more back again!
And he that will not follow Bourbon now,
Let him go hence, and with his cap in hand

---

54. **As I suck blood:** an oath—as truly as I am a bloodsucker! 56 ff. The Boy's soliloquy not only tells us of the sad fate of Bardolph and Nym, but gives us important information about the defenselessness of the English camp. 59. **roaring devil,** etc. The devil in the moralities was a very boisterous character, but was constantly worried by the Vice, or clown, who used to offer to pare his long nails with his dagger, which was palpably made of wood.—**that...his:** whose.
SCENE V.
1. **O diable!:** 'O the devil!' [A.C.] 2. **O Seigneur etc.:** 'O Lord. The day is lost, all is lost!' [A.C.] 3.**Mort de ma vie!:** 'Death of my life!' [A.C.] **confounded:** ruined, lost. 7. **perdurable:** lasting—practically, eternal.

	Like a base pander hold the chamber door	
	Whilst by a slave, no gentler than my dog,	15
	His fairest daughter is contaminated.	

CON.   Disorder, that hath spoil'd us, friend us now.
Let us on heaps go offer up our lives.

ORL.   We are enough yet living in the field
To smother up the English in our throngs,   20
If any order might be thought upon.

BOUR.   The devil take order now! I'll to the throng.
Let life be short; else shame will be too long.†   *Exeunt.*

SCENE VI. *Another part of the field.*

Alarum. Enter the King *and his* Train, [Exeter, *and others,*] *with* Prisoners.

KING   Well have we done, thrice-valiant countrymen;
But all's not done, yet keep the French the field.

EXE.   The Duke of York commends him to your Majesty.

KING   Lives he, good uncle? Thrice within this hour
I saw him down; thrice up again and fighting.   5
From helmet to the spur all blood he was.

EXE.   In which array, brave soldier, doth he lie,‡
Larding the plain; and by his bloody side,
Yoke-fellow to his honour-owing wounds,
The noble Earl of Suffolk also lies.   10
Suffolk first died; and York, all haggled over,
Comes to him, where in gore he lay insteep'd,
And takes him by the beard, kisses the gashes
That bloodily did yawn upon his face,
And cries aloud, 'Tarry, dear cousin Suffolk.   15
My soul shall thine keep company to heaven.

---

17. **friend:** befriend. 18. **on heaps:** in crowds.
SCENE VI.
3. **commends him:** sends his respects. 8. **Larding:** enriching—with his blood. 9. **honour-owing:** honour-possessing, honourable. 11. **haggled:** hacked and gashed.

---

† Both Olivier's and the BBC's versions end this scene with a terrified Dauphin afraid to ride back into battle. Branagh, on the other hand, has the Constable die in this scene after his last line, and gives Bourbon's lines to the enraged Dauphin, who is then shown fighting Henry. [A.C.]

‡ The death of York is the first time in the text that nobles are even reported to be fighting. Unsurprisingly, Branagh chooses to film the scene, replacing Exeter's speech with a grisly, slow-motion death, while Olivier cuts the speech entirely. [A.C.]

Tarry, sweet soul, for mine, then fly abreast;
As in this glorious and well-foughten field
We kept together in our chivalry.'
Upon these words I came and cheer'd him up.   20
He smil'd me in the face, raught me his hand,
And, with a feeble gripe, says 'Dear my lord,
Commend my service to my sovereign.'
So did he turn, and over Suffolk's neck
He threw his wounded arm and kiss'd his lips;   25
And so, espous'd to death, with blood he seal'd
A testament of noble-ending love.
The pretty and sweet manner of it forc'd
Those waters from me which I would have stopp'd;
But I had not so much of man in me,   30
And all my mother came into mine eyes
And gave me up to tears.

KING   I blame you not;
For, hearing this, I must perforce compound
With mistful eyes, or they will issue too.   *Alarum.*
But hark! what new alarum is this same?   35
The French have reinforc'd their scatter'd men.
Then every soldier kill his prisoners!
Give the word through.   *Exeunt.*

<hr>

SCENE VII. *Another part of the field.*

Enter Fluellen *and* Gower.

FLU.   Kill the poys and the luggage? 'Tis expressly against the law of arms.
        'Tis as arrant a piece of knavery, mark you now, as can be offert. In your
        conscience, now, is it not?   3

GOW.   'Tis certain there's not a boy left alive; and the cowardly rascals that ran
        from the battle ha' done this slaughter. Besides, they have burned and

<hr>

21. **raught:** reached. 23. **Commend my service:** give my love and duty. 31. **all my mother:** all the weakness that I inherited from my mother. Such apologies for weeping were a literary convention in Elizabethan English. 33. **I must perforce compound...issue too:** I am forced to make a compromise with my eyes, allowing them to be misty; otherwise they will insist on weeping outright. 35. **Alarum:** call to arms. This is the rally which the French nobles talk of in Scene v. 37. **kill his prisoners.** This order has been the focus of much critical debate–does Shakespeare mean us to see the King's command as justified or not and, even if justified, does it diminish the heroic nature of the victory? Perhaps the safest response is that it is an ambiguous moment that can be presented in many different ways on stage. [A.C.]

SCENE VII.
4. **not a boy left alive.** Falstaff's witty page, then, perished in this massacre. Thus, of the old retainers of Falstaff, Pistol is the sole survivor.

carried away all that was in the King's tent; wherefore the King most worthily hath caus'd every soldier to cut his prisoner's throat. O, 'tis a gallant king!

FLU. Ay, he was porn at Monmouth, Captain Gower. What call you the town's name where Alexander the Pig was born?   10

GOW. Alexander the Great.

FLU. Why, I pray you, is not 'pig' great? The pig, or the great, or the mighty, or the huge, or the magnanimous are all one reckonings, save the phrase is a little variations.

GOW. I think Alexander the Great was born in Macedon. His father was called Philip of Macedon, as I take it.   16

FLU. I think it is in Macedon where Alexander is porn. I tell you, Captain, if you look in the maps of the orld, I warrant you sall find, in the comparisons between Macedon and Monmouth, that the situations, look you, is both alike. There is a river in Macedon, and there is also moreover a river at Monmouth. It is call'd Wye at Monmouth; but it is out of my prains what is the name of the other river. But 'tis all one; 'tis alike as my fingers is to my fingers, and there is salmons in both. If you mark Alexander's life well, Harry of Monmouth's life is come after it indifferent well; for there is figures in all things. Alexander, God knows and you know, in his rages, and his furies, and his wraths, and his cholers, and his moods, and his displeasures, and his indignations, and also being a little intoxicates in his prains, did, in his ales and his angers, look you, kill his best friend, Cleitus.

GOW. Our King is not like him in that. He never kill'd any of his friends.   30

FLU. It is not well done, mark you now, to take the tales out of my mouth ere it is made and finished. I speak but in the figures and comparisons of it. As Alexander kill'd his friend Cleitus, being in his ales and his cups, so also Harry Monmouth, being in his right wits and his good judgments, turn'd away the fat knight with the great belly doublet. He was full of jests, and gipes, and knaveries, and mocks. I have forgot his name.   36

---

7. **'tis.** *It* was often applied familiarly to *persons*, either in contempt or (as here) in affection. 9. **at Monmouth.** Fluellen remembers with pride that King Henry was born in Wales. 12. **the pig,** etc. Fluellen is touchy when his English is corrected, and displays his knowledge by uttering a string of synonyms. 13. **maganimous:** great-souled, valiant. 14. **variations:** Fluellen's mistake for *various*. 24. **indifferent well:** pretty well. 25. **there is figures in all things:** either (1) there is a symbolic likeness in all the events of their lives, or (2) literal agreement must not be expected, for we must allow for figurative language in making such historical comparisons. The latter seems better and is borne out by l. 46: 'I speak but in the figures and comparisons of it.' 26. **in his rages,** etc. Fluellen remembers Gower's criticism of his English in l.11 and once more (as in l.12) displays his extensive knowledge of the English vocabulary. So also in l.26. 36. **Until this instant.** The King's anger is caused by the massacre of the non-combatants and the pillage of the camp.—**trumpet:** trumpeter. 'I will the banner from a trumpet take' (iv, 2, 61).

GOW.   Sir John Falstaff.

FLU.   That is he. I'll tell you there is good men porn at Monmouth.

GOW.   Here comes his Majesty.

> *Alarum. Enter* King Harry, [Warwick, Gloucester,
> Exeter, *and others*,] *with* Prisoners. *Flourish.*

KING   I was not angry since I came to France[†]   40
        Until this instant. Take a trumpet, herald;
        Ride thou unto the horsemen on yond hill.
        If they will fight with us, bid them come down,
        Or void the field. They do offend our sight.
        If they'll do neither, we will come to them   45
        And make them skirr away as swift as stones
        Enforced from the old Assyrian slings.
        Besides, we'll cut the throats of those we have;
        And not a man of them that we shall take
        Shall taste our mercy. Go and tell them so.   50

> *Enter* Montjoy [*the* Herald].

EXE.   Here comes the herald of the French, my liege.

GLOUC. His eyes are humbler than they us'd to be.

KING   How now? What means this, herald? Know'st thou not
        That I have fin'd these bones of mine for ransom?
        Com'st thou again for ransom?

HERALD   No, great King.   55
        I come to thee for charitable license
        That we may wander o'er this bloody field
        To look our dead, and then to bury them;
        To sort our nobles from our common men;
        For many of our princes (woe the while.)   60
        Lie drown'd and soak'd in mercenary blood;
        So do our vulgar drench their peasant limbs
        In blood of princes; and the wounded steeds
        Fret fetlock-deep in gore and with wild rage
        Yerk out their armed heels at their dead masters,   65

---

44. **void:** abandon. 46. **skirr:** scurry. 51. **liege:** liege lord. 54. **I have fin'd these bones of mine for ransom:** I have limited my ransom to these bones of mine—I will give no more. See iv, 3, 120 ff. The repetition of the word *ransom* in the next line gives the passage a scornful effect. 61. **mercenary blood:** the blood of common soldiers, who fight for wages.

---

† In Olivier's production, the murder of the boys leads Henry to challenge the Constable of France to a duel that effectively ends the war (see Introduction for a fuller description). [A.C.]

Killing them twice. O, give us leave, great King,
To view the field in safety and dispose
Of their dead bodies.

KING   I tell thee truly, herald,
I know not if the day be ours or no;
For yet a many of your horsemen peer   70
And gallop o'er the field.

HERALD   The day is yours.

KING   Praised be God and not our strength for it.
What is this castle call'd that stands hard by?

HERALD   They call it Agincourt.

KING   Then call we this the field of Agincourt,   75
Fought on the day of Crispin Crispianus.

FLU.   Your grandfather of famous memory, an't please your Majesty, and your
great-uncle Edward the Plack Prince of Wales, as I have read in the
chronicles, fought a most prave pattle here in France.

KING   They did, Fluellen.   80

FLU.   Your Majesty says very true. If your Majesties is remem'bred of it, the
Welshmen did good service in a garden where leeks did grow, wearing
leeks in their Monmouth caps; which your Majesty know to this hour is
an honourable badge of the service; and I do believe your Majesty takes
no scorn to wear the leek upon Saint Tavy's day.   85

KING   I wear it for a memorable honour;
For I am Welsh, you know, good countryman,

FLU.   All the water in Wye cannot wash your Majesty's Welsh plood out of your
pody, I can tell you that. God pless it and preserve it, as long as it pleases
his grace, and his majesty too!   90

KING   Thanks, good my countryman.

FLU.   By Jeshu, I am your Majesty's countryman, I care not who know it! I
will confess it to all the orld. I need not to be ashamed of your Majesty,
praised be God, so long as your Majesty is an honest man.

KING   God keep me so.

                    Enter Williams.

          Our heralds go with him.   95
Bring me just notice of the numbers dead

---

70. **peer:** appear, show themselves. 79. **pattle:** the Battle of Crécy. 83. **Monmouth caps:** a kind of cap
much worn by the Welsh. 86. **a memorable honour:** an honourable memorial. 88. **Welsh plood:** Henry
V's great-grandmother was a Welsh princess. 96. **just:** exact.

On both our parts.   [*Exeunt Heralds with Montjoy.*]
                        Call yonder fellow hither.

EXE.   Soldier, you must come to the King.

KING   Soldier, why wear'st thou that glove in thy cap?

WILL.   An't please your Majesty, 'tis the gage of one that I should fight withal, if
        he be alive.   101

KING   An Englishman?

WILL.   An't please your Majesty, a rascal that swagger'd with me last night; who,
        if 'a live and ever dare to challenge this glove, I have sworn to take him
        a box o' th' ear; or if I can see my glove in his cap, which he swore, as he
        was a soldier, he would wear (if alive), I will strike it out soundly.   106

KING   What think you, Captain Fluellen?
        Is it fit this soldier keep his oath?

FLU.   He is a craven and a villain else, an't please your Majesty, in my
        conscience.   110

KING   It may be his enemy is a gentleman of great sort, quite from the answer of
        his degree.

FLU.   Though he be as good a gentleman as the devil is, as Lucifer and Belzebub
        himself, it is necessary, look your Grace, that he keep his vow and his
        oath. If he be perjur'd, see you now, his reputation is as arrant a villain
        and a Jacksauce as ever his black shoe trod upon God's ground and his
        earth, in my conscience, law!   117

KING   Then keep thy vow, sirrah, when thou meet'st the fellow.

WILL.   So I will, my liege, as I live.

KING   Who serv'st thou under?   120

WILL.   Under Captain Gower, my liege.

FLU.   Gower is a good captain and is good knowledge and literatured in the
        wars.

KING   Call him hither to me, soldier.

WILL.   I will, my liege.   *Exit.* 125

KING   Here, Fluellen; wear thou this favor for me and stick it in thy cap. When
        Alençon and myself were down together, I pluck'd this glove from his

---

100. **should:** was to.—**withal:** with. 104. **take:** give. Cf. iv, 1, 177. 111. **quite from the answer of his**
degree: quite exempt from the necessity of accepting a challenge from a man of Williams' low rank. 116.
Jacksauce: saucy fellow. In his excitement Fluellen's English becomes even more uncertain than usual.
He uses *Jacksauce*, which is good English, in a very inappropriate way. 118. **sirrah:** merely *sir* with the *r*
'burred.' It is used as a familiar and sometimes a contemptuous term of address.

helm. If any man challenge this, he is a friend to Alençon and an enemy
to our person. If thou encounter any such, apprehend him, an thou dost
me love.   130

FLU.   Your Grace doe's me as great honours as can be desir'd in the hearts of his
subjects. I would fain see the man, that has but two legs, that shall find
himself aggrief'd at this glove, that is all. But I would fain see it once, an
please God of his grace that I might see.

KING   Know'st thou Gower?   135

FLU.   He is my dear friend, and please you.

KING   Pray thee go seek him and bring him to my tent.

FLU.   I will fetch him.   *Exit.*

KING   My Lord of Warwick, and my brother Gloucester,
Follow Fluellen closely at the heels.   140
The glove which I have given him for a favor
May haply purchase him a box o' th' ear;
It is the soldier's. I by bargain should
Wear it myself. Follow, good cousin Warwick.
If that the soldier strike him—as I judge   145
By his blunt bearing, he will keep his word—
Some sudden mischief may arise of it;
For I do know Fluellen valiant,
And, touch'd with choler, hot as gunpowder,
And quickly will return an injury.   150
Follow, and see there be no harm between them.
Go you with me, uncle of Exeter.   *Exeunt.*

SCENE VIII. *Before* King Henry's *pavilion.*

Enter Gower *and* Williams.

WILL.   I warrant it is to knight you, Captain.

Enter Fluellen.

FLU.   God's will and his pleasure, Captain, I beseech you now, come apace to
the King. There is more good toward you peradventure than is in your
knowledge to dream of.

WILL.   Sir, know you this glove?   5

FLU.   Know the glove? I know the glove is a glove.

---

129. **apprehend:** arrest. 149. **touched with choler:** when touched with anger. 150. **injury:** insult.

WILL.   I know this; and thus I challenge it.   *Strikes him.*

FLU.   'Sblood! an arrant traitor as any's in the universal world, or in France, or
in England!

GOW.   How now, sir? You villain!   10

WILL.   Do you think I'll be forsworn?

FLU.   Stand away, Captain Gower. I will give treason his payment into plows, I
warrant you.

WILL.   I am no traitor.

FLU.   That's a lie in thy throat. I charge you in his Majesty's name apprehend
him. He's a friend of the Duke Alençon's.   16

Enter Warwick *and* Gloucester.

WAR.   How now, how now? What's the matter?

FLU.   My Lord of Warwick, here is (praised be God for it!) a most contagious
treason come to light, look you, as you shall desire in a summer's day.
Here is his Majesty.   20

Enter King *and* Exeter.

KING   How now? What's the matter?

FLU.   My liege, here is a villain and a traitor that, look your Grace, has struck
the glove which your Majesty is take out of the helmet of Alençon.

WILL.   My liege, this was my glove, here is the fellow of it, and he that I gave it
to in change promis'd to wear it in his cap. I promis'd to strike him if he
did. I met this man with my glove in his cap, and I have been as good as
my word.   27

FLU.   Your Majesty hear now, saving your Majesty's manhood, what an arrant,
rascally, beggarly, lousy knave it is! I hope your Majesty is pear me
testimony and witness, and will avouchment, that this is the glove of
Alençon that your Majesty is give me, in your conscience, now.   31

KING   Give me thy glove, soldier. Look, here is the fellow of it.
'Twas I indeed thou promised'st to strike;
And thou hast given me most bitter terms.

SCENE VIII.
8. **'Sblood:** a very round oath; literally, 'by the blood of God.'—**in the universal world, or in France, or
in England.** Fluellen's excitement betrays him into an anti-climax. 15. **apprehend:** arrest. 18. **contagious:**
Fluellen probably means 'flagitious' or the like. 25. **in change:** in exchange. 28. **saving your Majesty's
manhood:** an apologetic phrase on account of the abusive words which Fluellen intends to use. The
meaning is, 'In what I say, I have no intention of insulting your honour.' Such phrases were common.
The literal meaning is, 'your manhood being safe,' i.e., unassailed, not infringed upon. 30. **avouchment.**
Fluellen uses this in place of the verb *avouch*, 'testify.' 34. **bitter terms:** bitter words.

FLU.	An please your Majesty, let his neck answer for it, if there is any martial law in the world. 36
KING	How canst thou make me satisfaction?
WILL.	All offenses, my lord, come from the heart. Never came any from mine that might offend your Majesty.
King	It was ourself thou didst abuse. 40
WILL.	Your Majesty came not like yourself. You appear'd to me but as a common man; witness the night, your garments, your lowliness. And what your Highness suffer'd under that shape, I beseech you take it for your own fault, and not mine; for had you been as I took you for, I made no offense. Therefore I beseech your Highness pardon me. 45
KING	Here, uncle Exeter, fill this glove with crowns And give it to this fellow. Keep it, fellow, And wear it for an honor in thy cap Till I do challenge it. Give him the crowns; And, Captain, you must needs be friends with him. 50
FLU.	By this day and this light, the fellow has mettle enough in his belly. Hold, there is twelve pence for you; and I pray you to serve God, and keep you out of prawls, and prabbles, and quarrels, and dissensions, and, I warrant you it is the better for you.
WILL.	I will none of your money. 55
FLU.	It is with a good will. I can tell you it will serve you to mend your shoes. Come, wherefore should you be so pashful? Your shoes is not so good. 'Tis a good silling, I warrant you, or I will change it.
	Enter [an English] Herald.
KING	Now, herald, are the dead numb'red?
HER.	Here is the number of the slaught'red French. *[Gives a paper.]* 60
KING	What prisoners of good sort are taken, uncle?
EXE.	Charles Duke of Orleans, nephew to the King; John Duke of Bourbon and Lord Bouciqualt: Of other lords and barons, knights and squires, Full fifteen hundred, besides common men. 65

---

41. **like yourself:** in your own attire, etc. 44. **I made no offense.** A regular Elizabethan idiom, like 'to make a fault.' 51. **By this day,** etc. As soon as Fluellen knows that it was all the King's joke, his resentment is pacified.53. **prawls,** etc. Fluellen's supply of synonyms still holds out. 55. **I will none of your money.** Williams is something of a grumbler and not so easily pacified as the more mercurial Fluellen. 57. **wherefore should you be so pashful?** Fluellen takes the soldier's reluctance to be the result of modesty. It is not clear in the end that Williams takes the shilling. [A.C.]

KING   This note doth tell me of ten thousand French
        That in the field lie slain. Of princes, in this number,
        And nobles bearing banners, there lie dead
        One hundred twenty-six; added to these,
        Of knights, esquires, and gallant gentlemen,   70
        Eight thousand and four hundred; of the which,
        Five hundred were but yesterday dubb'd knights;
        So that in these ten thousand they have lost
        There are but sixteen hundred mercenaries;
        The rest are princes, barons, lords, knights, squires,   75
        And gentlemen of blood and quality.
        The names of those their nobles that lie dead:
        Charles Delabreth, High Constable of France;
        Jaques of Chatillon, Admiral of France;
        The master of the crossbows, Lord Rambures;   80
        Great Master of France, the brave Sir Guichard Dauphin;
        John Duke of Alençon; Anthony Duke of Brabant,
        The brother to the Duke of Burgundy;
        And Edward Duke of Bar; of lusty earls,
        Grandpré and Roussi, Fauconberg and Foix,   85
        Beaumont and Marle, Vaudemont and Lestrale.
        Here was a royal fellowship of death.
        Where is the number of our English dead?
                            [*Herald gives another paper.*]
        Edward the Duke of York, the Earl of Suffolk,
        Sir Richard Ketly, Davy Gam, Esquire;   90
        None else of name, and of all other men
        But five-and-twenty. O God, thy arm was here.
        And not to us, but to thy arm alone,
        Ascribe we all. When, without stratagem,
        But in plain shock and even play of battle,   95
        Was ever known so great and little loss
        On one part and on th' other? Take it, God,
        For it is only thine.

EXE.   'Tis wonderful.

KING   Come, go we in procession to the village;
        And be it death proclaimed through our host   100
        To boast of this, or take that praise from God
        Which is his only.

---

66. **note:** list, memorandum. 74. **mercenaries:** common soldiers. See note on iv, 6, 61. 92. **But five-and-twenty.** This absurd number is actually handed down in the chronicles. 97. **Take it, God:** i.e., take the honour of it. 99. **in procession:** in religious procession.

FLU.	Is it not lawful, an please your Majesty, to tell how many is kill'd?
KING	Yes, Captain, but with this acknowledgment,
	That God fought for us.

That God fought for us.   105

FLU.	Yes, my conscience, he did us great good.
KING	Do we all holy rites.

Let there be sung '*Non nobis*' and '*Te Deum*,'
The dead with charity enclos'd in clay,
And then to Calais; and to England then;†   110
Where ne'er from France arriv'd more happy men.   *Exeunt.*

ACT FIVE

Enter Chorus.

Vouchsafe to those that have not read the story‡
That I may prompt them; and of such as have,
I humbly pray them to admit th' excuse
Of time, of numbers, and due course of things
Which cannot in their huge and proper life   5
Be here presented. Now we bear the King
Toward Calais. Grant him there. There seen,
Heave him away upon your winged thoughts
Athwart the sea. Behold, the English beach
Pales in the flood with men, with wives and boys,   10
Whose shouts and claps outvoice the deep-mouth'd sea,
Which, like a mighty whiffler fore the King,
Seems to prepare his way. So let him land,
And solemnly see him set on to London.

---

103. Is it not lawful, etc. Fluellen, whose Welsh valour is mingled with an equally Welsh fondness for boasting, is a little distressed at the thought that the army is to take no credit for itself. 108. **'Non nobis' and 'Te Deum':** two well-known Psalms.

ACT V. PROLOGUE.
What the Chorus is about to say is necessary information for those in the audience who have not read the history. For those who have, it may serve as a reminder of what is omitted on account of the impossibility of presenting all the details in the theater. 10. **Pales in:** encloses as with a palisade. 12. **whiffler:** a person who went before the procession to clear the way. Here the sea seems in a similar manner to announce the coming of King Henry. 14. **set on:** advancing.

---

† Branagh closes this scene with a long tracking shot of the King carrying the dead Boy through the battlefield, and then cuts directly to 5.2, preserving the solemn mood. [A.C.]

‡ In the nineteenth century, this speech was often replaced or at least augmented by a processional with dozens of extras and Henry mounted on a real horse. In the twentieth century, this speech was often cut. [A.C.]

So swift a pace hath thought that even now   15
You may imagine him upon Blackheath;
Where that his lords desire him to have borne
His bruised helmet and his bended sword
Before him through the city. He forbids it,
Being free from vainness and self-glorious pride;   20
Giving full trophy, signal, and ostent
Quite from himself to God. But now behold,
In the quick forge and working house of thought,
How London doth pour out her citizens.
The Mayor and all his brethren in best sort—   25
Like to the senators of th' antique Rome,
With the plebeians swarming at their heels—
Go forth and fetch their conqu'ring Cæsar in;
As, by a lower but loving likelihood,
Were now the general of our gracious Empress,   30
As in good time he may, from Ireland coming,
Bringing rebellion broached on his sword,
How many would the peaceful city quit
To welcome him! Much more, and much more cause,
Did they this Harry. Now in London place him;   35
As yet the lamentation of the French
Invites the King of England's stay at home;
The Emperor's coming in behalf of France
To order peace between them; and omit
All the occurrences, whatever chanc'd,   40
Till Harry's back-return again to France.
There must we bring him, and myself have play'd

---

21. **trophy, signal, and ostent.** These three words mean much the same thing, but the first is the most definite. The second, meaning any kind of *evidence* or *sign* of victory, is somewhat less specific; and the third, *ostent*, meaning *show*, is the most abstract of all. We have here a fine example of the reversed climax. 22. **from:** the emphatic *from*, meaning 'away from.' 23. **In the quick forge,** etc.: i.e., in your imaginations. 25. **in best sort:** in their finest array, and with due ceremony. 26. **ántique.** Accented on the first syllable, according to Schmidt's rule. 29. **by a lower but loving likelihood:** to use a comparison which is somewhat less in dignity than the thing compared, but which nevertheless we use to show our love. The general referred to in l. 30 is Essex, who was now in Ireland attempting to subdue a rebellion. Since Essex was not so high a person as King Henry and the Irish wars were not so important as the French, the comparison is, of course, a lower one, but its employment testifies to the love which the writer has for Essex. As a matter of fact, Essex's return was quite different from that here hoped for. 30. **Empress.** A title much affected by Queen Elizabeth. Thus Spenser dedicates his *Faerie Queene* to her under this designation. 32. **broached:** spitted—as if rebellion were a monster which Essex was bringing home on the very sword which had pierced it. 36, 37. **the lamentation of the French Invites the King of England's stay at home:** i.e., the French are in such despair that there is no occasion for King Henry to show himself in France at present. 38. **The Emperor:** i.e., the Holy Roman Emperor. 39. **To order peace:** to arrange terms of peace. 42. **There must we bring him.** This prepares the audience for the place of the next scenes, namely, France, and gives them to understand that in the meantime the King has returned to England and gone back to France again.

The interim, by rememb'ring you 'tis past.
Then brook abridgment; and your eyes advance,
After your thoughts, straight back again to France.   *Exit.*   45

SCENE I. *France. The English camp.*

Enter Fluellen *and* Gower.

GOW.   Nay, that's right. But why wear you your leek to-day? Saint Davy's day is
        past.   2

FLU.   There is occasions and causes why and wherefore in all things. I will tell
        you ass my friend, Captain Gower. The rascally, scauld, beggarly, lousy,
        pragging knave, Pistol—which you and yourself and all the world know
        to be no petter than a fellow, look you now, of no merits—he is come to
        me and prings me pread and salt yesterday, look you, and bid me eat my
        leek. It was in a place where I could not breed no contention with him,
        but I will be so bold as to wear it in my cap till I see him once again, and
        then I will tell him a little piece of my desires.   10

Enter Pistol.

GOW.   Why, here he comes, swelling like a turkey cock.

FLU.   'Tis no matter for his swellings nor his turkey cocks. God pless you,
        Aunchient Pistol! you scurvy, lousy knave, God pless you!

PIST.   Ha! art thou bedlam? Dost thou thirst, base Trojan,
        To have me fold up Parca's fatal web?   15
        Hence! I am qualmish at the smell of leek.

FLU.   I peseech you heartily, scurvy, lousy knave, at my desires, and my requests,
        and my petitions, to eat, look you, this leek. Because, look you, you do

---

43. **Remembering you:** reminding you. 44. **brook abridgment:** put up with or be indulgent to our
cutting down the full history.
SCENE I.
1. **Nay, that's right.** As so often is the case, we hear only the end of the conversation. These two words
refer to something which Fluellen has said; we have no means of knowing what. 4. **Ass:** Fluellen means
as, which would ordinarily be spelled in Elizabethan English as we spell it. The spelling *ass* here indicates
that he pronounced it *ass*, and so appeared to call Captain Gower by a very uncomplimentary name. 7.
yesterday: i.e., on St. David's Day, when the leek was worn, as was customary on that day. St. David is the
patron saint of the Welsh. 8. **It was in a place where I could,** etc. An example of such a place would be
in the King's presence, in which it was improper for persons to engage in a private quarrel; but we need
not suppose that this is what was meant here. There would be many other occasions on which it would
be undignified and bad discipline for Fluellen to resent Pistol's insult. 14. **art thou bedlam?** art thou a
lunatic? Pistol has misconstrued Fluellen's forbearance of the previous day and regards him as a coward.
15. **Fold up Parca's fatal web:** i.e., put an end to their life. The Parcæ were the Roman Fates. Pistol thinks
of them here as weaving the web of a man's life. To *fold up* this web would then be 'to abbreviate the life.'

not love it, nor your affections and your appetites and your disgestions doo's not agree with it, I would desire you to eat it.   20

PIST.   Not for Cadwallader and all his goats.

FLU.   There is one goat for you.   (*Strikes him.*)
Will you be so good, scauld knave, as eat it?

PIST.   Base Trojan, thou shalt die!   24

FLU.   You say very true, scauld knave, when God's will is. I will desire you to live in the meantime, and eat your victuals. Come, there is sauce for it. [*Strikes him.*] You call'd me yesterday mountain-squire, but I will make you today a squire of low degree. I pray you fall to. If you can mock a leek, you can eat a leek.

GOW.   Enough, Captain. You have astonish'd him.   30

FLU.   I say I will make him eat some part of my leek, or I will peat his pate four days.—Bite, I pray you. It is good for your green wound and your ploody coxcomb.

PIST.   Must I bite?

FLU.   Yes, certainly, and out of doubt, and out of question too, and ambiguities.   36

PIST.   By this leek, I will most horribly revenge! I eat, and yet, I swear—

FLU.   Eat, I pray you. Will you have some more sauce to your leek? There is not enough leek to swear by.

PIST.   Quiet thy cudgel. Thou dost see I eat.   40

FLU.   Much good do you, scauld knave, heartily. Nay, pray you throw none away. The skin is good for your broken coxcomb. When you take occasions to see leeks hereafter, I pray you mock at 'em; that is all.

PIST.   Good.

FLU.   Ay, leeks is good. Hold you, there is a groat to heal your pate.   45

PIST.   Me a groat?

---

19. **affections:** likings.—**disgestions:** digestions- not a blunder of Fluellen's, for the form was common. 21. **Cadwallader:** Cadwallader the Great, the last of the Welsh Kings, whom Pistol here takes pleasure in representing as a goatherd merely. Of course, this is an insult to all Welshmen. 27. **mountain-squire:** i.e., a poverty-stricken squire from the barren mountains of Wales. 28. **squire of low degree:** an allusion to a very popular metrical romance, composed in the fifteenth century and well-known in Shakespeare's time. Of course Fluellen means that he will humble Pistol. 30. **astonished:** almost equivalent to 'stunned.' 31, 32. **four days.** *Four* was a common round number.—**ploody coxcomb:** bloody head. *Coxcomb* is a jocose and contemptuous name for 'head.' 41. **Much good do you:** a common blessing with one's meat. 42. **broken coxcomb.** Note that *to break one's head* was simply 'to draw blood upon one's head'—not, of course, 'to fracture the skull.'

FLU. Yes, verily and in truth, you shall take it, or I have another leek in my pocket, which you shall eat.

PIST. I take thy groat in earnest of revenge.

FLU. If I owe you anything, I will pay you in cudgels. You shall be a woodmonger and buy nothing of me but cudgels. God b' wi' you, and keep you, and heal your pate.   *Exit.* 52

PIST. All hell shall stir for this!

GOW. Go, go. You are a counterfeit cowardly knave. Will you mock at an ancient tradition, begun upon an honorable respect and worn as a memorable trophy of predeceased valor, and dare not avouch in your deeds any of your words? I have seen you gleeking and galling at this gentleman twice or thrice. You thought, because he could not speak English in the native garb, he could not therefore handle an English cudgel. You find it otherwise; and henceforth let a Welsh correction teach you a good English condition. Fare ye well.   *Exit.* 61

PIST. Doth Fortune play the huswife with me now?
News have I, that my Nell is dead i' th' spital
Of malady of France,
And there my rendezvous is quite cut off.   65
Old I do wax, and from my weary limbs
Honor is cudgell'd. Well, bawd will I turn,
And something lean to cutpurse of quick hand.
To England will I steal, and there I'll steal;
And patches will I get unto these cudgell'd scars   70
And swear I got them in the Gallia wars.   *Exit.*

---

49. **I take thy groat in earnest of revenge.** *Earnest* is properly a small sum of money paid on the conclusion of a bargain to bind the transaction. Here, of course, Pistol means that he takes this money to remind him that he owes Fluellen revenge. 51. **God b' wi' you:** one of the numerous contracted forms of *God be with you* meaning 'good-bye.' The most contracted of all is that which we at present use, *good-bye* itself. 55. **upon an honourable respect:** on account of an honourable reason or consideration. 57. **gleeking:** poking fun.—**galling:** making satirical remarks. *To gall* is properly 'to excoriate' or 'to rub the skin off.' 59. **garb:** fashion. 61. **condition:** character. The meaning is, 'teach you how a good Englishman should behave.' 62. **play the huswife:** i.e., play the hussy, betray me. Fortune is constantly spoken of as an unfaithful mistress because she smiles upon all men but is constant to none. 63. **my Nell:** this would seem to be the Hostess. The Folios read 'Doll.' The correction is Capell's.—**spital:** hospital. 66, 67. **from my weary limbs Honor is cudgell'd:** having been publicly cudgelled without instantly killing his assailant, Pistol's honour as a gentleman and a soldier was of course quite gone.—**bawd:** pander. 68. **something lean to cutpurse of quick hand:** i.e., show a certain inclination to the profession of Nimblefinger Cutpurse. This profession, as well as that of pandering, had been cultivated by Pistol before he went to the wars.

SCENE II. *France. The* French King's *Palace.*

Enter, at one door, King Henry, Exeter, Bedford, [Gloucester,] Warwick, [Westmoreland,] *and other* Lords; *at another,* Queen Isabel, *the* [French] King, *the* Duke of Burgundy, [*the* Princess Katherine, Alice,] *and other* French.

KING	Peace to this meeting, wherefore we are met.	
	Unto our brother France and to our sister	
	Health and fair time of day. Joy and good wishes	
	To our most fair and princely cousin Katherine.	
	And as a branch and member of this royalty,	5
	By whom this great assembly is contriv'd,	
	We do salute you, Duke of Burgundy.	
	And, princes French, and peers, health to you all.	
FRANCE	Right joyous are we to behold your face,	
	Most worthy brother England. Fairly met.	10
	So are you, princes English, every one.	
QUEEN	So happy be the issue, brother England,†	
	Of this good day and of this gracious meeting	
	As we are now glad to behold your eyes—	
	Your eyes which hitherto have borne in them,	15
	Against the French that met them in their bent,	
	The fatal balls of murdering basilisks.	
	The venom of such looks, we fairly hope,	
	Have lost their quality, and that this day	
	Shall change all griefs and quarrels into love.	20
KING	To cry amen to that, thus we appear.	
QUEEN	You English princes all, I do salute you.	
BURG.	My duty to you both, on equal love,	
	Great Kings of France and England. That I have labor'd	
	With all my wits, my pains, and strong endeavors	25
	To bring your most imperial Majesties	

SCENE II.
2. **France:** the King of France. 5. **royalty:** royal family. 16. **met them in their bent:** met them in their gaze. 17. **The fatal balls of murdering basilisks.** This line involves an elaborate double meaning. (1) The basilisk was a fabulous monster of the serpent kind, which was supposed to kill by venomous emanations from its eyeballs, so that its glance meant death. (2) The name *basilisk* was also given to a certain kind of cannon, so called because originally it bore the figure of a basilisk. 19. **quality:** nature, essential quality.—**that.** The clause depends upon *hope* in the line before. 20. **griefs:** grievances. 23. **on equal love:** in consequence of the equal love that I bear to you both.

---

† Branagh chooses to cut Queen Isabel and either cut or reassign her lines. In a play that is so concerned with "claiming from the female" it is worth considering the effect of his decision on an audience. [A.C.]

Unto this bar and royal interview,
Your mightiness on both parts best can witness.
Since, then, my office hath so far prevail'd
That, face to face and royal eye to eye,   30
You have congreeted, let it not disgrace me
If I demand, before this royal view,
What rub or what impediment there is
Why that the naked, poor, and mangled Peace,
Dear nurse of arts, plenty, and joyful births,   35
Should not, in this best garden of the world,
Our fertile France, put up her lovely visage.
Alas, she hath from France too long been chas'd.
And all her husbandry doth lie on heaps,
Corrupting in it own fertility.   40
Her vine, the merry cheerer of the heart,
Unpruned dies; her hedges even-pleach'd,
Like prisoners wildly overgrown with hair,
Put forth disorder'd twigs; her fallow leas
The darnel, hemlock, and rank fumitory   45
Doth root upon, while that the coulter rusts
That should deracinate such savagery.
The even mead, that erst brought sweetly forth
The freckled cowslip, burnet, and green clover,
Wanting the scythe, all uncorrected, rank,   50
Conceives by idleness and nothing teems
But hateful docks, rough thistles, kecksies, burrs,
Losing both beauty and utility.
And as our vineyards, fallows, meads, and hedges,
Defective in their natures, grow to wildness,   55
Even so our houses and ourselves and children
Have lost, or do not learn for want of time,
The sciences that should become our country;
But grow like savages, as soldiers will,

---

27. **Unto this bar.** There was a bar fixed between the French dignitaries and the English when the interview actually took place, and we must suppose that this was also represented on the stage. 29. **my office:** my good offices, my services. 31. **congreeted:** met together. 32. **before this royal view:** in the presence of these King s. 33. **rub:** an impediment—a technical term in bowling. 37. **put up her lovely visage:** i.e., raise it from the ground where she lies prostrate; or, perhaps, simply show her face, since the idea seems to be that she has been driven out of France. 42. **even-pleached:** even-plaited—i.e., with the ends twined in so as to present an even surface, as was often done with hedges. 44. **fallow leas:** unplanted fields. 45. **darnel:** the weeds mentioned in the Bible. 47. **deracinate:** uproot.—**savagery:** wild growths. 48. **erst:** formerly. The word is really a superlative from the same root from which comes the comparative form *ere*. 49. **burnet:** a kind of fodder. 51. **Conceives by idleness:** that is to say, is fertilized with useless weeds.—**teems:** brings forth. The object is *nothing*. 52. **kecksies:** a kex is a dry hemlock shoot or the like. 55. **Defective in their natures:** i.e., losing their true natures, which is to bring forth useful plants, and the like.

That nothing do but meditate on blood,   60
To swearing and stern looks, defus'd attire,
And everything that seems unnatural.
Which to reduce into our former favor
You are assembled, and my speech entreats
That I may know the let why gentle Peace   65
Should not expel these inconveniences
And bless us with her former qualities.

KING   If, Duke of Burgundy, you would the peace
            Whose want gives growth to th' imperfections
            Which you have cited, you must buy that peace   70
            With full accord to all our just demands;
            Whose tenures and particular effects
            You have, enschedul'd briefly, in your hands.

BURG.   The King hath heard them; to the which as yet
            There is no answer made.

KING   Well then, the peace,   75
            Which you before so urg'd, lies in his answer.

FRANCE   I have but with a cursorary eye
            O'erglanc'd the articles. Pleaseth your Grace
            To appoint some of your Council presently
            To sit with us once more, with better heed   80
            To resurvey them, we will suddenly
            Pass our accept and peremptory answer.

KING   Brother, we shall. Go, uncle Exeter,
            And brother Clarence, and you, brother Gloucester,
            Warwick, and Huntingdon, go with the King;   85
            And take with you free power to ratify,
            Augment, or alter, as your wisdoms best
            Shall see advantageable for our dignity,
            Anything in or out of our demands;

---

61. **defused:** disordered. 63. **favour:** good appearance, comeliness. 65. **the let:** the hindrance. 66. **inconveniences:** improper or unbecoming things. 68. **would:** here used as a transitive verb—if you would like to have. 73. **enschedul'd:** drawn up in the form of a schedule 77. **cursorary:** cursory. 78. **Pleaseth your Grace:** a common polite form, equivalent to 'if your Grace pleases' or 'may it please your Grace.' 79. **presently:** at once. 81. **suddenly:** immediately,—containing the notion of rapidity without that of abruptness. 82. **Pass our accept,** etc. A peremptory answer—'settle upon what we can accept and give an answer which shall be final so far as we are concerned.' For this use of *pass* cf. 'to pass a law,' 'to pass a degree of rank.' 83. **we shall.** A most courteous form of assent in Elizabethan times—more so than 'we will,' because it does not imply, as the latter does, the exercise of any volition on the part of the person who consents. 88. **advantageable:** advantageous. 89. **in or out of our demands:** whether included in our demands or not. 90. **consign:** agree formally. *To consign* literally means 'to seal together with' and so 'to consent in a most solemn way.' 93. **Happily:** very likely, perhaps. 94. **When articles too nicely urged be**

| | And we'll consign thereto. Will you, fair sister, | 90 |
| | Go with the princes or stay here with us? | |

QUEEN   Our gracious brother, I will go with them.
Happily a woman's voice may do some good
When articles too nicely urg'd be stood on.

KING   Yet leave our cousin Katherine here with us.   95
She is our capital demand, compris'd
Within the fore-rank of our articles.

QUEEN   She hath good leave.

> *Exeunt, all except King Henry, Katherine,*
> *and the Gentlewoman [Alice].*

KING   Fair Katherine, and most fair!
Will you vouchsafe to teach a soldier terms[†]
Such as will enter at a lady's ear   100
And plead his love suit to her gentle heart?

KATH.   Your Majesty shall mock at me. I cannot speak your England.

KING   O fair Katherine, if you will love me soundly with your French heart, I will be glad to hear you confess it brokenly with your English tongue. Do you like me, Kate?   105

KATH.   *Pardonnez-moi*, I cannot tell vat is 'like me.'

KING   An angel is like you, Kate, and you are like an angel.

KATH.   *Que dit-il? Que je suis semblable à les anges?*

ALICE.   *Oui, vraiment, sauf vostre grâce, ainsi dit-il.*

KING   I said so, dear Katherine, and I must not blush to affirm it.   110

KATH.   *O bon Dieu! les langues des hommes sont pleines de tromperies.*

KING   What says she, fair one? that the tongues of men are full of deceits?

ALICE   *Oui*, dat de tongues of de mans is be full of deceits. Dat is de Princesse.

KING   The Princess is the better English-woman. I' faith, Kate, my wooing is fit for thy understanding. I am glad thou canst speak no better English; for

---

stood on: When things or demands, the mention of which is too punctilious or particular, are insisted on or made a point of. Note that *urged* means not 'pressed' (which is the sense of *stood on*) but simply 'mentioned'—a common meaning. *Nicely* means 'scrupulously,' 'punctiliously,' 'with too great attention to detail,' or 'an inclination to insist on trifles.' 108. 'What does he say? That I am like the angels?' 109. 'Yes, truly, saving your Grace, that is what he says.' 110. 'Oh, good God, the tongues of men are full of deceit.' 114. **The Princess is the better Englishwoman:** i.e., she has a true English modesty and common sense in the matter of trusting compliments.

---

† This scene plays equally well as a romantic wooing and as a tense, enforced negotiation, depending on the tone of voice of Henry and especially Katherine. [A.C.]

Fig. 4: Olivier's Henry woos a flirtatious Katherine—she glances up at him coyly and they hold hands—making this a purely romantic scene. © United Artists / Photofest.

if thou couldst, thou wouldst find me such a plain king that thou wouldst think I had sold my farm to buy my crown. I know no ways to mince it in love but directly to say 'I love you.' Then, if you urge me farther than to say, 'Do you in faith?' I wear out my suit. Give me your answer; i' faith, do! and so clap hands and a bargain. How say you, lady?   120

KATH.   *Sauf vostre honneur*, me understand well.

KING   Marry, if you would put me to verses or to dance for your sake, Kate, why, you undid me. For the one I have neither words nor measure; and for the other I have no strength in measure, yet a reasonable measure in strength. If I could win a lady at leapfrog, or by vaulting into my saddle with my armour on my back, under the correction of bragging be it spoken, I should quickly leap into a wife. Or if I might buffet for my love, or bound my horse for her favours, I could lay on like a butcher and sit like a jackanapes, never off. But, before God, Kate, I cannot look greenly nor gasp out my eloquence, nor I have no cunning in protestation; only

---

116. **such a plain king** . As a matter of fact, the King was highly accomplished. He was anything but a farmer-like person. We have our choice, then, in the present case between two suppositions. Either Shakespeare (1) is describing a different kind of man from Prince Hal or (2) the King is representing himself as far plainer than he actually is. 117. **to mince it:** to mince matters, to speak delicately, like a courtier. 119. **I wear out my suit:** I have used up my resources as a wooer. 120. **clap hands:** clasp hands. 121. 'Saving your honor.' 122. **you undid me:** you would ruin me. 124. **in measure:** a measure was a kind of stately court dance. 126. **under the correction of bragging be it spoken:** an apologetic phrase, 'let me speak it without incurring blame for bragging, for I do not mean to brag.' 127, 128. **buffet:** box.—**bound my horse:** make my horse jump. 129. **jackanapes:** ape. The reference is, of course, to performing apes that ride horseback.—**look greenly:** look foolish. The King's contemptuous phrase for the moonstruck, sentimental looks of lovers. 130. **cunning:** skill.

Fig. 5: Branagh's Henry woos a reluctant Katherine—she turns away from him and looks serious, even sad, reminding the audience that she is being forced to marry a conqueror. © Samuel Goldwyn Company / Photofest.

downright oaths, which I never use till urg'd, nor never break for urging. If thou canst love a fellow of this temper, Kate, whose face is not worth sun-burning, that never looks in his glass for love of anything he sees there, let thine eye be thy cook. I speak to thee plain soldier. If thou canst love me for this, take me; if not, to say to thee that I shall die, is true—but for thy love, by the Lord, no; yet I love thee too. And while thou liv'st, dear Kate, take a fellow of plain and uncoined constancy; for he perforce must do thee right, because he hath not the gift to woo in other places. For these fellows of infinite tongue that can rhyme themselves into ladies' favors, they do always reason themselves out again. What! A speaker is but a prater; a rhyme is but a ballad. A good leg will fall, a straight back will stoop, a black beard will turn white, a curl'd pate will grow bald, a fair face will wither, a full eye will wax hollow; but a good heart, Kate, is the sun and the moon; or rather, the sun, and not the moon, for it shines bright and never changes, but keeps his course truly. If thou would have such a one, take me; and take me, take a soldier; take a soldier, take a

132, 133. **whose face is not worth sun-burning;** i.e., whose complexion is so rugged that the sun takes no pleasure in spoiling it. 134. **let thine eye be thy cook:** the meaning of this phrase, which sounds proverbial, can only be guessed, but it must have been familiar to the Elizabethans. A cook takes plain material and dresses it until it forms an attractive dish. The King's face, he says, is plain. Let the Princess love him and that face will become attractive in her eyes. Thus her eyes may be said to invest his face with qualities which it does not possess by nature, as the cook prepares plain material by the exercise of his art. Other meanings are possible, but this seems to be the best.—**I speak to thee plain soldier:** i.e., the language that I use to thee is plain soldier's talk. 137. **uncoined:** sincere, uncounterfeited. A *coiner* was a false coiner or counterfeiter. 138. **do thee right:** be faithful to thee. 141. **will fall:** will fall away, will shrink. 145. **his:** its.

king. And what say'st thou then to my love? Speak, my fair—and fairly, I
pray thee.   148

KATH.   Is it possible dat I sould love de enemie of France?

KING   No, it is not possible you should love the enemy of France, Kate; but in
loving me you should love the friend of France; for I love France so well
that I will not part with a village of it—I will have it all mine. And, Kate,
when France is mine and I am yours, then yours is France and you are
mine.

KATH.   I cannot tell vat is dat.   155

KING   No, Kate? I will tell thee in French; which I am sure will hang upon
my tongue like a new-married wife about her husband's neck, hardly to
be shook off. *Quand j'ai la possession de France, et quand vous avez la
possession de moi* (Let me see, what then? Saint Denis be my speed!), *donc
vostre est France et vous estes mienne.* It is as easy for me, Kate, to conquer
the kingdom as to speak so much more French. I shall never move thee in
French, unless it be to laugh at me.   162

KATH.   *Sauf vostre honneur, le François que vous parlez, il est meilleur que l'Anglois
lequel je parle.*

KING   No, faith, is't not, Kate. But thy speaking of my tongue, and I thine, most
truly-falsely, must needs be granted to be much at one. But, Kate, dost
thou understand thus much English? Canst thou love me?   167

KATH.   I cannot tell.

KING   Can any of your neighbours tell, Kate? I'll ask them. Come, I know thou
lovest me; and at night when you come into your closet, you'll question
this gentlewoman about me; and I know, Kate, you will to her dispraise
those parts in me that you love with your heart; but, good Kate, mock me
mercifully; the rather, gentle Princess, because I love thee cruelly. If ever
thou beest mine, Kate—as I have a saving faith within me tells me thou
shalt—I get thee with scambling, and thou must therefore needs prove
a good soldier-breeder. Shall not thou and I, between Saint Denis and
Saint George, compound a boy, half French, half English, that shall go to
Constantinople and take the Turk by the beard? Shall we not? What say'st
thou, my fair flower-de-luce?

KATH.   I do not know dat.   180

---

150. **you should love:** you would certainly love. 159. **Saint Denis.** The King swears appropriately enough
by the national saint of France. 163. 'Saving your honor, the French you speak is better than the English
I speak.' 171. **dispraise:** mock (falsely, as a game). 174. **a saving faith.** A common religious expression.
175. **scambling:** struggling (i.e., war). 178. **the Turk:** the Grand Turk, the Sultan. 179: **flower-de-luce:**
the *fleur-de-lys,* emblem of France.

KING   No; 'tis hereafter to know, but now to promise. Do but now promise, Kate, you will endeavor for your French part of such a boy; and for my English moiety take the word of a king and a bachelor. How answer you, *la plus belle Katherine du monde, mon très-cher et devin déesse?*

KATH.   Your Majestee ave fausse French enough to deceive de most sage damoisell dat is en France.   186

KING   Now, fie upon my false French! By mine honor in true English, I love thee, Kate; by which honor I dare not swear thou lovest me; yet my blood begins to flatter me that thou dost, notwithstanding the poor and untempering effect of my visage. Now beshrew my father's ambition! He was thinking of civil wars when he got me; therefore was I created with a stubborn outside, with an aspect of iron, that, when I come to woo ladies, I fright them. But in faith, Kate, the elder I wax, the better I shall appear. My comfort is, that old age, that ill layer-up of beauty, can do no more spoil upon my face. Thou hast me, if thou hast me, at the worst; and thou shalt wear me, if thou wear me, better and better; and therefore tell me, most fair Katherine, will you have me? Put off your maiden blushes; avouch the thoughts of your heart with the looks of an empress; take me by the hand, and say 'Harry of England, I am thine!' which word thou shalt no sooner bless mine ear withal but I will tell thee aloud 'England is thine, Ireland is thine, France is thine, and Henry Plantagenet is thine'; who, though I speak it before his face, if he be not fellow with the best king, thou shalt find the best king of good fellows. Come, your answer in broken music, for thy voice is music and thy English broken, therefore, queen of all Katherines, break thy mind to me in broken English. Wilt thou have me?   206

KATH.   Dat is as it sall please de *roi mon père*.

KING   Nay, it will please him well, Kate. It shall please him, Kate.

KATH.   Den it sall also content me.

KING   Upon that I kiss your hand and I call you my queen.   210

KATH.   *Laissez, mon seigneur, laissez, laissez! Ma foi, je ne veux point que vous abaissiez vostre grandeur en baisant la main d'une de vostre seigneurie indigne serviteur. Excusez-moi, je vous supplie, mon très-puissant seigneur.*

KING   Then I will kiss your lips, Kate.

---

183. **bachelor:** young fellow, young knight. 184. 'most beautiful Katherine in the world, my very dear and divine goddess'. 189. **blood:** inclination, natural impulse. 190. **untempering:** unattractive. *To temper* often means 'to influence,' 'to work to one's will.' The King means that his face is not 'winning.' — **beshrew:** confound, curse. 192. **stubborn:** rude, rough. 198. **avouch:** declare. 200. **withal:** with. 205. **break:** broach, utter. 207. **roi mon père:** 'the king, my father'. 211-213. 'Let be, my lord, let be, let be! By my faith, I do not at all wish to abase your greatness in kissing the hand of one who is your lordship's humble servant. Excuse me, I beg you, my most mighty lord.'

KATH.   *Les dames et demoiselles pour estre baisées devant leur noces, il n'est pas la*
          coutume de France.   216

KING   Madam my interpreter, what says she?

ALICE   Dat it is not be de fashon pour de ladies of France—I cannot tell vat is
          '*baiser*' en Anglish.

KING   To kiss.   220

ALICE   Your Majestee *entendre* bettre *que moi.*

KING   It is not a fashion for the maids in France to kiss before they are married,
          would she say?

ALICE   *Oui, vraiment.*

KING   O Kate, nice customs curtsy to great kings. Dear Kate, you and I cannot
          be confin'd within the weak list of a country's fashion. We are the makers
          of manners, Kate, and the liberty that follows our places stops the mouth
          of all find-faults, as I will do yours for upholding the nice fashion of your
          country in denying me a kiss. Therefore patiently, and yielding. [*Kisses
          her.*] You have witchcraft in your lips, Kate. There is more eloquence in
          a sugar touch of them than in the tongues of the French Council, and
          they should sooner persuade Harry of England than a general petition of
          monarchs. Here comes your father.

                    Enter the French Power *and the* English Lords.

BURG.   God save your Majesty! My royal cousin,
          Teach you our princess English?   235

KING   I would have her learn, my fair cousin, how perfectly I love her, and that
          is good English.

BURG.   Is she not apt?

KING   Our tongue is rough, coz, and my condition is not smooth, so that, having
          neither the voice nor the heart of flattery about me, I cannot so conjure
          up the spirit of love in her that he will appear in his true likeness.   241

BURG.   Pardon the frankness of my mirth if I answer you for that. If you would
          conjure in her, you must make a circle; if conjure up love in her in his true
          likeness, he must appear naked and blind. Can you blame her then, being
          a maid yet ros'd over with the virgin crimson of modesty, if she deny the
          appearance of a naked blind boy in her naked seeing self? It were, my
          lord, a hard condition for a maid to consign to.

KING   Yet they do wink and yield, as love is blind and enforces.

215-216. 'The women and girls do not kiss before marriage, it is not the custom of France.' 221.
entendre...que moi: 'listens...than me.' 224. 'Yes, exactly.' 255. **nice:** precise, punctilious. 226. **list:**
barrier. 239. **condition:** character, ways.

BURG.	They are then excus'd, my lord, when they see not what they do.
KING	Then, good my lord, teach your cousin to consent winking. 250
BURG.	I will wink on her to consent, my lord, if you will teach her to know my meaning. For maids well summer'd and warm kept are like flies at Bartholomew-tide, blind, though they have their eyes, and then they will endure handling which before would not abide looking on.
KING	This moral ties me over to time and a hot summer; and so I shall catch the fly, your cousin, in the latter end, and she must be blind too. 256
BURG.	As love is, my lord, before it loves.
KING	It is so; and you may, some of you, thank love for my blindness, who cannot see many a fair French city for one fair French maid that stands in my way. 260
FRANCE	Yes, my lord, you see them perspectively—the cities turn'd into a maid, for they are all girdled with maiden walls that war hath never ent'red.
KING	Shall Kate be my wife?
FRANCE	So please you. 265
KING	I am content, so the maiden cities you talk of may wait on her. So the maid that stood in the way for my wish shall show me the way to my will.
FRANCE	We have consented to all terms of reason.
KING	Is't so, my lords of England? 270
WEST.	The King hath granted every article: His daughter first, and in sequel, all, According to their firm proposed natures.
EXE.	Only he hath not yet subscribed this: Where your Majesty demands that the King of France, having any occasion to write for matter of grant, shall name your Highness in this form and with this addition, in French, *Nostre trèscher fils Henri, Roi d'Angleterre, héritier de France*; and thus in Latin, *Praecarissimus filius noster Henricus, Rex Angliae et haeres Franciae*.

252-253. **flies at Bartholomew-tide.** A proverb. 259. **cannot see many a fair French city,** etc.: he means that, out of his love for Katherine, he is willing to give up many French cities which he might possess. 261. **perspectively:** as through a perspective glass—a kind of optical toy which distorts objects. It was in great favour with the Elizabethans and is often mentioned. 273. **According to their firm proposed natures:** exactly as they were defined in the terms proposed. 274. **Where:** whereas. 276. **in:** out of, for. The common causal *in* used in adjurations. —**addition:** title. 277-279. 'our very dear son Henry, King of England, heir of France'.

FRANCE	Nor this I have not, brother, so denied	280
	But your request shall make me let it pass.	
KING	I pray you then, in love and dear alliance,	
	Let that one article rank with the rest,	
	And thereupon give me your daughter.	
FRANCE	Take her, fair son, and from her blood raise up	285
	Issue to me, that the contending kingdoms	
	Of France and England, whose very shores look pale	
	With envy of each other's happiness,	
	May cease their hatred, and this dear conjunction	
	Plant neighborhood and Christianlike accord	290
	In their sweet bosoms, that never war advance	
	His bleeding sword 'twixt England and fair France.	
LORDS	Amen.	
KING	Now, welcome, Kate, and bear me witness all	
	That here I kiss her as my sovereign queen. *Flourish.*	295
QUEEN	God, the best maker of all marriages,	
	Combine your hearts in one, your realms in one!	
	As man and wife, being two, are one in love,	
	So be there 'twixt your kingdoms such a spousal	
	That never may ill office, or fell jealousy,	300
	Which troubles oft the bed of blessed marriage,	
	Thrust in between the paction of these kingdoms	
	To make divorce of their incorporate league;	
	That English may as French, French Englishmen,	
	Receive each other. God speak this Amen.	305
ALL	Amen!	
KING	Prepare we for our marriage; on which day,†	
	My Lord of Burgundy, we'll take your oath,	
	And all the peers', for surety of our leagues.	
	Then shall I swear to Kate, and you to me,	310
	And may our oaths well kept and prosp'rous be. *Sennet. Exeunt.*	

---

284. **daughter.** Some think the final *r* was trilled so as to make up the otherwise missing syllable at the end of the verse. 291. **that never war advance:** in order that war may never lift up. 296. **God, the best maker of all marriages.** According to the proverb 'Marriages are made in heaven.' 300. **ill office:** any unfriendly act.—**fell:** cruel. 302. **paction:** agreement. 311. **Sennet:** a trumpet flourish, indicating a ceremonial exit or entrance.

---

†   Both the BBC and Olivier's version present a stylized marriage at this point (the BBC is here echoing Olivier), and Olivier returns the action to the Globe, with the actors taking their bows at the end of the play. [A.C.]

EPILOGUE

Enter Chorus.

Thus far, with rough and all-unable pen,
Our bending author hath pursu'd the story,
In little room confining mighty men,
Mangling by starts the full course of their glory.
Small time, but in that small, most greatly lived   5
This star of England. Fortune made his sword;
By which the world's best garden he achieved,
And of it left his son imperial lord.
Henry the Sixth, in infant bands crown'd King
Of France and England, did this king succeed,   10
Whose state so many had the managing
That they lost France and made his England bleed;
Which oft our stage hath shown, and for their sake
In your fair minds let this acceptance take.   *[Exit.]*

EPILOGUE.
2. **bending:** bending over his desk; or, better, bending under the weight of the subject. 3. **room:** space. 4. **Mangling by starts,** etc.: depicting their glorious careers in disconnected fragments—as it were, by fits and starts. 7. **achieved:** won. 9. **infant bands:** swaddling clothes. Henry V died 2 months before Charles VI of France, and Henry VI became king of England and France before he was a year old. 11. **had the managing:** i.e., had the managing *of.* The preposition at the end of a clause is often omitted in Elizabethan English. Since Henry VI was too young to rule on his own, his many uncles fought over who should be regent. 13. **which oft our stage hath shown:** an allusion to the popularity of the three parts of *King Henry VI.*—**for their sake:** for the sake of those plays.

How to Read
Henry V as Performance

Shakespeare's plays are wonderful pieces of literature, full of beautiful images and powerful language. And most often, they are taught as literature, read silently at home, or discussed piece by piece in the classroom. But what a reader needs to know about Shakespeare, and about plays in general, is that plays are not like other types of writing. Plays offer only part of the final product–the dialogue and a few stage directions. Because of this, the best way to fully experience a play is through a performance, live or on film. However, many times that is not possible, and even when it is, reading is still a valuable experience. It is not always easy to see performances. Some plays aren't staged very often, and when they are they can be expensive to attend. Furthermore, when you see a play, you are seeing the director's version. When you read a play, you can be your own director and imagine the characters and set however you wish. But there are certain techniques all readers must use to get full enjoyment out of reading a Shakespearean play.

The first technique for reading a Shakespearean play successfully is to familiarize yourself with it before you start. Shakespeare wrote over 400 years ago, and therefore things he would have assumed his audience knew may be completely unfamiliar now. So the more information you can gather before you begin, the more you will understand. A good place is to determine what the play's *genre* is.

Shakespeare wrote three genres: comedies, tragedies and histories. *Henry V* is a history, and that means that the play will concern the actions of kings and other nobles, a war or at least some battles, as well as people trying to gain or keep power. Knowing the play is a history gives a reader a basic framework, and some idea of what to expect. If you want more information, it is always a good idea to read the introduction, especially with a history. This is because Shakespeare expected that his audience would know what happened before and after the events of the individual play. He built in reminders, but without the basic background, these reminders won't make much sense. For example, in 4.1, Henry V prays to God to "think not upon the fault/My father made in compassing the crown./I Richard's body have interred new." Unless you know that Henry V's father stole the throne from the rightful king, Richard II, this prayer will make little sense. So take the time to read the introduction, or use other resources to understand the setting, time period and background of the play's events.

Another thing people often rush past is the list of characters, which is printed at the beginning of the play. It is worth looking at this list to get an idea of how the characters are related to each other. The list for *Henry V*, for example, tells us that the Duke of Exeter is uncle to the king, the Dukes of Gloucester and Bedford are his brothers and the Duke of York is his cousin. So we know that all the dukes are closely related to the king, and it makes more sense, in 1.2, when he asks their advice. But the relationships also tell us something else: the relative ages of these characters. Since the English throne goes to the eldest son, we know that Gloucester and Bedford are younger than Henry V, and we know that Exeter is older, possibly a good deal older. That can give you an idea of the way the characters look and how they act towards each other.

When you have read the introduction and character list, you will have a good basic idea of what the play is about. But all this information will only help you understand it, not make it come alive. In order for that to happen, you need to actively imagine what is happening. You have to create a "theater of the mind." As you read, imagine what the characters look like, how they are dressed and what their surroundings are like. Take the time at the beginning of each scene to imagine what the setting is like. Cast the characters, maybe even using your favorite movie stars. Try reading important speeches in a variety of ways to see which one you like best, and if the different ways can help you uncover different meanings in the scene.

For example, the very first scene in *Henry V* is simply one man—a Chorus—speaking directly to the audience. He is apologizing for presenting such important events as Henry's invasion of France on stage, on "this unworthy scaffold" where there are no horses, armies or kings to do justice to the story. How do you imagine this man is dressed? Where is he standing? In 1944, Laurence Olivier made a film of *Henry V* and recreated Elizabethan England and the Globe Theater for the first few scenes, so that he could show the Chorus apologizing to the original audience. In 1989, Kenneth Branagh made another version of the play, and he chose to have the Chorus in modern dress, wandering around an empty movie set. While very different, both of these options visually underscore the focus of the speech—however sophisticated the illusion, it cannot match real life.

After you have created the scene in your mind, be alert to what are called *implicit stage directions*. While Shakespeare did not leave many notes about what the actors should do, there are many places where the dialogue refers to actions. These can help guide you in imagining the action. For example, in 1.2 the Ambassador from France tells Henry that the Dauphin has sent him a "tun of treasure." Henry says, "What treasure, uncle?" to which Exeter responds "Tennis balls, my liege." From these lines we know that the "treasure" must be in some sort of closed box (because Henry cannot see what it is) and that Exeter must open it. However it is up to the director or the reader to decide how big the box is (is it a literal ton?) and how Exeter reacts when he opens it. In Olivier's version, the box is huge (it takes two men to carry it in) and very brightly colored. Exeter opens the box and is so shocked he immediately shuts it again. In Branagh's version, the box is small, made of dark wood. Exeter opens it and takes out a tennis ball, looking at it grimly before he announces what the "treasure" is.

There are other places in *Henry V* where being an active participant in creating the play will help you understand it. There are several scenes where taking the time to read closely and imagine the scene in detail will reveal layers of meaning that just understanding the words will not. These are not, by any means, the only important scenes, but here are some suggestions of places to look closely and imagine yourself as the director.

1.1 is a scene that comes alive in the acting. Why would Shakespeare begin with this conference between two churchmen who will not reappear after 1.2? What are their attitudes towards the King, the French and the proposed bill? How are these things related? One purpose of this scene is to tell the audience that things have changed since the end of Shakespeare's play *Henry IV:2*, when we last saw Henry, but there are other maneuvers going on as well. Olivier and Branagh approach this scene from completely opposite points: Olivier makes the scene purely comic, while Branagh films the two men whispering in a dark room, plotting how to use war to distract the king from domestic matters.

Another way imagination is important is that it can fill in what Shakespeare leaves out, or at least leaves out of the dialogue. For example, in 3.3, Henry delivers terrible threats to the Governor of Harfleur, telling him that if the city does not surrender, Henry and his men will torture and kill all the inhabitants. If the audience sees Henry's obvious relief when the town surrenders, they will realize that Henry was bluffing. This silent action presents a very different Henry than if the threats are presented as something he would actually carry out.

A much bigger version of imagining what Shakespeare leaves out is the battle of Agincourt, because there are no actual scenes of battle. While it is true that Shakespeare's company couldn't present a full-fledged battle with horses and thousands of men, there are plenty of plays in which battles are represented by duels, or groups of men fighting. An audience might expect to see a duel between Henry and the Dauphin, considering that the Dauphin has been taunting Henry since Act 1. Instead, the only battle scenes are Pistol taking a Frenchman hostage, the French nobles' amazement at the way the battle is going, and Henry hearing about his brother's death and then ordering the killing of all the French prisoners. As a director, it is worth considering why Shakespeare didn't show any actual fighting, even if you think your version should have an actual battle scene (as both film versions of the play have).

Another thing you might notice is that Katherine, Alice and Monsieur le Fer, a French soldier, speak either broken English or French. Resist the temptation to go straight for the translation in the footnotes, and ask yourself what it would have been like for Shakespeare's audience to hear these foreign words in the middle of the play. Why would Shakespeare do this? You'll quickly notice that all of the important dialogue is translated, so that Shakespeare made sure the audience could follow the scenes, while allowing for a lot of humor when one character doesn't understand another. But you might also notice that all the noble male French characters speak perfect English. Only a foot soldier and the women are unable to communicate well. You might consider that, in addition to providing some humor, Shakespeare is making a comment about certain characters. What do a French soldier and a French princess have in common? Well, both are ordered to do things they might not want to do (fight in a war, marry an enemy) and neither has any choice in the matter. You might further consider why both Olivier and Branagh cut the scene with Pistol and Monsieur le Fer, but keep the scenes with Katherine.

It is in answering questions like those above that understanding how to read a play begins to shade into understanding how to interpret a play. When you play out scenes in your head, and take the time to decide how you think characters should look and dress and act, you begin to see connections that simply aren't apparent from simply reading the words on the page. Not only will you have more fun and understand the play better, you will develop your own interpretation. In fact, you will make the play your own.

Annalisa Castaldo

Timeline for the History Plays
(relevant plays in parentheses)

1399: Forced abdication of Richard II; Henry IV becomes king (*Richard II*)

This disruption in orderly succession sets the stage for almost 100 years of infighting and civil war among the nobles, all of whom trace their right to the throne back to Richard's grandfather, Edward III.

1413: Henry V, oldest son of Henry IV, takes the throne on his father's death (*2 Henry IV*)

1415: Battle of Agincourt (*Henry V*)

1420: Henry is named heir of France and marries Katherine, daughter of Charles VI (*Henry V*)

In Shakespeare's version, the French capitulation and marriage of Henry and Katherine appear to follow directly from the battle of Agincourt, but in fact there were five more years of fighting.

1422: Henry V dies prematurely and is succeeded by his nine-month-old son, Henry VI

Because Henry VI is so young, the kingdom is ruled by his uncles and cousins, who cannot agree and fight amongst themselves for personal gain.

Charles IV dies and Henry VI is crowned king of France

Henry V's widow marries Owen Tudor

Their grandson, Henry Tudor, will eventually become king.

1429: Joan of Arc begins freeing France from English control (*1 Henry VI*)

1445: Henry VI marries Margaret of Anjou (*2 Henry VI*)

Henry gives up control of some parts of France as part of the marriage settlement. This unpopular move causes rival factions at court, leading directly to civil war.

1450: By this date, all English-held French territories except the port town of Calais are retaken by the French

1455:   First battle of the civil war later dubbed the Wars of the Roses (*3 Henry IV*)

    The two sides are the Lancasters (allied with Henry VI and represented by red roses) and the Yorks (allied with the Duke of York, cousin of Henry VI, and represented by white roses)

1461:   Edward of York deposes Henry VI and is crowned Edward IV (*3 Henry VI*)

1470:   Henry VI is restored briefly to the throne (*3 Henry VI*)

1471:   Henry VI is murdered and Edward IV regains the throne (*3 Henry VI*)

1483:   Edward IV dies, succeeded by his 12-year-old son, Edward V (*Richard III*)

    Richard III takes the throne (*Richard III*)

    Edward V and his brother Richard are housed in the Tower of London and never seen again.

    In *Richard III*, Richard usurps the throne purely for personal gain, but there is historical evidence that he was motivated by fears of further civil war if a child was crowned.

1485:   Battle of Bosworth field, Henry Tudor (son of Edmund Tudor, half brother of Henry VI) defeats Richard III and is crowned Henry VII (*Richard III*)

    Henry VII begins the Tudor line and becomes the great grandfather of Elizabeth I, the reigning monarch when Shakespeare composed his history plays.

1513:   *The Prince* written by Niccolo Machiavelli: In sixteenth century England, the "Machiavel" was understood as an amoral power seeker who used deceit and violence to succeed. A model for Richard III, and, some critics argue, Henry V.

1564:   William Shakespeare born in Stratford-upon-Avon to John and Mary Shakespeare

1567-:   The opening of the Red Lion Playhouse, the first public playhouse in England.

1582:   William Shakespeare marries Anne Hatthaway (November)

1583:   Birth of Shakespeare's daughter, Susanna (baptised May 26th)

1585:   Birth of Shakespeare's son, Hamnet, and daughter, Judith (baptized February 2nd)

1592:   Robert Greene's *A Groat's Worth of Wit Bought with a Million of Repentance*, refers to Shakespeare as an "upstart crow."

    We do not know exactly when Shakespeare left Stratford for England; the seven years between the birth of the twins and Greene's attack are often called the "lost years." There is much speculation on what Shakespeare did during this time and why he left his wife and children to join the theater in London.

1592-94: Plague years. Theaters closed. Shakespeare wrote his poems and many of his sonnets during this period.

1594: William Shakespeare and Richard Burbage become sharers in the Lord Chamberlain's Men, a company of actors, reorganized when the theaters reopen after the Plague.

Shakespeare would later become a major shareholder in the theater and this, rather than publication of his plays, is how he made his money.

1596: Burial of Hamnet Shakespeare, August 11th, in Stratford.

No record exists of Shakespeare's feelings at the loss of his only son.

1599: Robert Devereux, the Earl of Essex, returns from a failed military campaign in Ireland. The lines of praise in *Henry V* (5.Chorus.30-33) for Essex's assumed triumph date that play to before September 1599.

1603: Death of Elizabeth. James VI of Scotland (b. 1566) crowned King James I of England.

The Lord Chamberlain's Men, recognized as the premier acting troupe in England, become the King's Men. Plays such as *Macbeth* and *The Winter's Tale* are written with King James in mind.

c.1611: Shakespeare retires to Stratford

1616: Death of William Shakespeare (April 23rd).

1623: Publication of the *First Folio*

Without this effort of his friends to collect his works, eighteen of Shakespeare's plays would have been lost.

TOPICS FOR DISCUSSION AND FURTHER STUDY

Critical Issues

1. Do you feel the war against France is justified? Why or why not?

2. Notice all the different kinds of English that are spoken. For example, the lower-class characters in 2.1 speak with one kind of accent, the four captains in 3.2 all have different accents and Katherine speaks yet another kind of "English." Why do you think Shakespeare focused so intently on creating different accents? Can you draw correlations between the kind of English characters speak and the amount of power they have?

3. Henry's justification of war is based on his descent from a French princess— "claiming from the female." Look for other instances where mothers are invoked or presented. What view of women is presented by the play?

4. Notice how many things in this play are reported, rather than dramatized— the attempted conspiracy, the death of Falstaff, the hanging of Bardolph, the whole battle of Agincourt, the death of York, and the killing of the prisoners. You could also include Henry's threats before Harfluer, since they are never carried out. Why does so little *happen* in this play? What reason could Shakespeare have for reporting rather than showing?

5. Does Henry intend to carry out his threats before Harfleur? If the governor had not surrendered, do you think Henry would have ordered/allowed his men to rape and kill the civilians? If you have never considered it before, how does it change your opinion of Henry if you believe he is serious in his threats?

6. Compare the French camp scene (4.2) and the English camp scene (4.3). How does Shakespeare create sympathy for the English? Is he as successful at creating dislike for the French? Considering the fact that the French will lose 10,000 men to the English twenty-nine, is it fair to bias the audience?

7. Are Henry's arguments to Williams in 4.1 convincing? Is the King responsible for the men who fight for him? In Henry's "Upon the king" soliloquy he says the only thing he has that ordinary men do not is ceremony. Is this true? What does Henry mean by "ceremony"?

8. Study the St. Crispin's Day speech (4.3), which is widely considered a masterpiece. What is powerful about it? Notice that Henry does not actually address the problem (the lack of men), but instead focuses on future rewards. Is this an effective strategy? How could you use this strategy today?

9. This play is the fourth of a tetraology—four works closely linked together—yet *Henry V* is most often read and staged alone. Is the play successful alone? Are the references to characters like Falstaff and Richard II confusing? How much help did you need to understand the events of the play?

10. Are the shifts between history, epic and comedy in the play confusing? Do the comic scenes with Pistol and company detract from the serious elements of the play? Why or why not?

Performance Issues

1. If you were directing a film of *Henry V* who would you pick to play Henry, and why? How does the physical appearance of the character influence the audience's perception of that character?

2. Both Laurence Olivier and Kenneth Branagh chose to include the Battle of Agincourt, despite the fact that Shakespeare did not write any actual fight scenes. Why do you think Shakespeare left out the battle? Why did Olivier and Branagh decide to include it? What does actually seeing the battle add to the audience's understanding of or reaction to the play?

3. Olivier's version of *Henry V* was made in 1944 during World War II. Why did he chose to make a film of this play, specifically, at this time? Discuss how the reality of war may have influenced Olivier's directing (for example, the bloodless and colorful battle, or the removal of the traitors).

4. Find a scene or part of a scene that has been left out of one of the film versions. Why do you think the director chose to leave it out? What is the effect of this deletion? If the scene is included in the other version, discuss the differences that result. Do you prefer having the scene or not?

5. Both Olivier and Branagh keep the Chorus, despite the fact that with film technology there is no need to apologize for a lack of spectacle. Why do you think they keep the Chorus?

6. The film *Renaissance Man* involves an unemployed advertising agent teaching Shakespeare to a bunch of army recruits. Most of the film features *Hamlet*, but towards the end the recruits go to see a production of *Henry V* and later one recites the St. Crispin's Day speech. Why does the film change from *Hamlet* to *Henry V*? How does the film use *Henry V*?

7. If possible, watch the BBC or RSC television production of *Henry V*. How do these productions differ from the two film versions? Both of these productions are much more complete than either film? How does this affect the characterizations and themes, compared to the films?

BIBLIOGRAPHY

Editor's note: This bibliography represents both classic and new works of scholarship that are generally accessible to advanced high school and all college students. The bibliography offers a range of theoretical approaches and methods of study. In all cases, I have attempted to provide the best or first work in a specific area. [A.C.]

Altman, Joel. "'Vile Participation': The Amplification of Violence in the Theater of *Henry V*." *Shakespeare Quarterly* 42:1 (1991): 1-32

Altman argues that scholars have ignored the specific material aspects of the play's first performances (one of the few plays we can date with certainty). This is one of the best modern readings for understanding the ambiguity of the play and the title character.

Baldo, Jonathan. "Wars of Memory in *Henry V*" *Shakespeare Quarterly* 47:2 (1996): 132-59.

Focuses on the importance of memory within the play and the call to remember that the play provides to the audience. A reading that incorporates the Elizabethan culture and history without simplification.

Brennan, Anthony. *Henry V* (Harvester New Critical Introductions to Shakespeare). Hemel Hempstead: Harvester Wheatsheaf, 1992.

This text provides a solid introduction to all facets of the play, with up-to-date but accessible criticism.

Danson, Lawrence. "*Henry V*: King, Chorus, and Critics." *Shakespeare Quarterly* 34 (1983): 27-43.

Discusses the importance of the Chorus and the reason Shakespeare includes such elaborate apologies in this specific play.

Dollimore, John and Alan Sinfield, "History and Ideology: The Instance of *Henry V*" in *Alternative Shakespeares*. John Drakakis, ed. London: Methuen & Co., 1985, 206-27.

A dense essay which argues that *Henry V* is not only ambiguous in its representation of power, but also in its consideration of ideology itself, and how ideology was presented on the stage.

Eggert, Katherine. "Nostalgia and the Not Yet Late Queen: Refusing Female Rule in *Henry V*" *ELH* 61:3 (1994): 523-50.

This article intelligently considers the play's obsession with female rule and how male power originates from women.

Greenblatt, Stephen. "Invisible Bullets: Renaissance Authority and Its Subversion, *Henry IV* and *Henry V*" in *Political Shakespeare: New Essays in Cultural Materialism*. John Dollimore and Alan Sinfield, eds. Manchester, Manchester University Press, 1985, 18-47.

Classic article of New Historicism, linking Shakespeare's play to colonial ambitions in the New World.

McEachern, Claire. "*Henry V* and the Paradox of the Body Politic" *Shakespeare Quarterly* 45:1 (1994): 33-56.

This essay approaches the play's central character through an examination of subjectivity, and what makes Henry seem both like a person and personable, that is, likeable.

Newman, Karen. *Fashioning Femininity and English Renaissance Drama*. Chicago: University of Chicago Press, 1991.

Newman devotes a chapter to *Henry V* in which she suggests that femininity and foreignness are linked, and that Katherine is silenced when Henry woos her into "Englishness."

Norwich, John Julius. *Shakespeare's Kings: The Great Plays and the History of England in the Middle Ages: 1337-1485*. New York: Simon & Schuster, 1999.

Discusses Shakespeare's portrayal in relation to the history. Provides both excellent historical background and discussion of how the play relates to actual events.

Pilkington, Ace G. *Screening Shakespeare. From Richard II to Henry V*. Newark, DE: University of Delaware Press, 1991.

Looks at the performances of Shakespeare's histories on screen in the twentieth century. The only book that focuses exclusively on film versions of the histories.

Rabkin, Norman. "Rabbits, Ducks, and *Henry V.*" *Shakespeare Quarterly* 28 (1977): 279-96.

Rabkin refutes the idea that the play must be read as either an uncomplicated celebration or a cynical rejection of Henry and his use of power. Instead, Rabkin argues convincingly that the play offers both readings at the same time.

Smith, Emma (ed). *King Henry V* (Shakespeare in Production). Cambridge: Cambridge University Press, 2002.

This series provides a detailed background on various productions, both stage and screen, as well as footnotes specifically geared towards performative rather than textual issues. An excellent text to use for any work on *Henry V* as drama.

Taylor, Gary. *Three Studies in the Text of Henry V.* Oxford: Claredon Press, 1979.

One of the first serious studies of the textual variations in the play and how they matter to understanding and performance.

Tillyard, E.M. *W. Shakespeare's History Plays.* Harmondsworth: Penguin, 1962.

The creation of the popular "Elizabethan world view," which suggests that Elizabethans, and by extension Shakespeare, believed that history was divinely ordained and strictly ordered. A classic if conservative reading of Shakespeare's view of history.

FILMOGRAPHY

Henry V (1944). Dir. Laurence Olivier. With Laurence Olivier, Robert Newton, Leslie Banks, Renee Asherson, Leo Genn. 137 minutes. DVD release 1999.

> DVD extras: Commentary by Film Historian Bruce Eder - Shakespearean Royalty: A Chronology of England's Rulers - Stills Galleries: the Book of Hours, production photos.

> Olivier's version of the play simplifies Henry's character and the war, but offers a three-staged version of reality that begins in Shakespeare's Globe for the "premier" of *Henry V*.

Henry V (1980). Dir. David Giles. With David Gwillim, Rob Edwards, Martin Neil. 163 minutes. Also sold as part of the BBC *Shakespeare Histories* Box.

> Much more complete and faithful to the text than either of the two studio films, the BBC version is unfortunately also lower in production values. Because it strives to present Shakespeare "straight" this version does not offer a strong interpretation of either the main character or the ambiguities of the text, presenting them to the viewer unadorned.

Henry V (1989). Dir. Kenneth Branagh. With Kenneth Branagh, Derek Jacobi, Ian Holm, Judi Dench, Paul Scofield. 138 minutes. DVD release 1990.

> Post-Vietnam, Branagh offers a darker version of Shakespeare's play that emphasizes the personal cost of war, but nevertheless sees Henry as heroic. The film focuses on Henry's growth as a man and as a king during the course of the war.

Star Trek: The Next Generation episode #58 "Defector" (1987). Dir. Larry Shaw. With Patrick Stewart and Brent Spiner. 60 minutes.

> In the opening sequence Data, under Picard's supervision, reenacts Henry's speech on ceremony from Act 3. Picard later quotes from the play. Data's performance is clearly based on Olivier.

Renaissance Man (1994). Dir. Penny Marshall. With Danny DeVito, Gregory Hines, Ed Begley Jr. and Mark Wahlberg. 128 minutes. DVD release 2003.

    An unemployed advertising executive uses Shakespeare to teach Army recruits. Although the film focuses on *Hamlet*, the teacher takes the recruits to see a production of *Henry V* and one recruit responds to his sergeant's taunting by reciting the St. Crispin's Day speech.

The Wars of the Roses (1990). Dir. Michael Bogdanov. With Michael Pennington, Michael Cronin, Paul Brennen, Barry Stanton, Andrew Jarvis. 176 minutes.

    Part of a series by the English Theatre Company which filmed staged productions of all of Shakespeare's Wars of the Roses history plays.